Workbook
Street Law
A Course in Practical Law

Fifth Edition

By
Margaret Armancas-Fisher
University of Puget Sound
Institute for Citizen Education in the Law

Edited by
Lee P. Arbetman, M.Ed., J.D.
Adjunct Professor of Law
Georgetown University Law Center

Edward L. O'Brien, J.D.
Adjunct Professor of Law
Georgetown University Law Center

*A Publication of the National Institute
for Citizen Education in the Law*

West Publishing Company
Minneapolis/St. Paul   New York   Los Angeles   San Francisco

WEST'S COMMITMENT TO THE ENVIRONMENT

In 1906, West Publishing Company began recycling materials left over from the production of books. This began a tradition of efficient and responsible use of resources. Today, up to 95% of our legal books and 70% of our college texts and school texts are printed on recycled, acid-free stock. West also recycles nearly 22 million pounds of scrap paper annually—the equivalent of 181,717 trees. Since the 1960s, West has devised ways to capture and recycle waste inks, solvents, oils, and vapors created in the printing process. We also recycle plastics of all kinds, wood, glass, corrugated cardboard, and batteries, and have eliminated the use of Styrofoam book packaging. We at West are proud of the longevity and the scope of our commitment to the environment.

Production, Prepress, Printing and Binding by West Publishing Company.

 *TEXT IS PRINTED ON 10% POST CONSUMER RECYCLED PAPER*

Table of Contents

Chapter 4, Consumer Law

Chapter 5, Family Law

Chapter 6, Housing Law

Chapter 7, Individual Rights and Liberties

The National Institute for Citizen Education in the Law

Street Law is a product of the National Institute for Citizen Education in the Law (NICEL). The Institute grew out of a Georgetown University Law Center program, launched in 1971, in which law students teach practical law courses in District of Columbia high schools, juvenile and adult correctional institutions, and a number of community-based settings.

NICEL was created to promote increased opportunities for citizen education in the law. It develops curricula, trains teachers, and replicates programs. It also provides technical assistance and curriculum materials to law schools, school systems, departments of corrections, juvenile justice agencies, bar associations, legal service and community organizations, state and local governments, and other groups and individuals interested in establishing law-related education programs. Through its national clearinghouse, NICEL distributes lists of its materials and services as well as technical assistance papers that guide practitioners in the replication of its programs models. NICEL also provides assistance for programs at the elementary school level.

Some NICEL programs have also been replicated in South Africa, Hungary, Chile, Bolivia, Ecuador, and the Philippines.

In addition the *Street Law*, the Institute's publications include
   Democracy for All (1994)
   We Can Work It Out: Problem Solving through Mediation (1993)
   Human Rights for All (1993)
   Teens, Crime, and the Community (1992)
   Practical Law for Jail and Prison Personnel (1987)
   Great Trials in American History: Civil War to the Present (1985)
   Current Legal Issues Filmstrip Series (1985)
   Family Law: Competencies in Law and Citizenship (1984)
   Street Law: Mock Trial Manual (1984)
   Current Legal Issues Filmstrip Series (1984)
   Street Law Filmstrip Series (1983)
   Consumer Law: Competencies in Law and Citizenship (1982)
   Law and the Consumer (1982)

For further information or assistance, please contact
    National Institute for Citizen Education in the Law
    711 G Street, S.E.
    Washington, D.C. 20003
    (202) 546-6644
    FAX (202) 546-6649
    TT (202) 546-7591

Street Law Supplements

The **Street Law** instructional program consists of *Street Law: A Course in Practical Law, Fifth Edition,* plus the following carefully designed, integrated supplements available to all adopters:

Teacher's Manual — This manual includes answers to all in-text questions, many suggested activities and community resources, mock trials, and comments about the new questions posed to the student reader in the text photo captions.

Test Bank — The test bank contains a variety of question for every section of every chapter. All answers are provided, including model answers for short-answer questions. The test bank is also available in computerized form. New to this edition are authentic assessment instruments and their accompanying rubrics that define the performance level at each stage of a student's development.

Workbook — A new feature of the program, the workbook was developed by Washington's LRE coordinator Margaret Armancas-Fisher, of the University of Puget Sound. It contains many varied worksheets including a number that promote higher order thinking skills.

Handbook of Selected Court Cases — This casebook contains original source material from important Supreme Court decisions as reported by West Publishing's WESTLAW Division. A citation, introduction, WESTLAW summary, excerpt, and decision is provided for each case.

Street Law: Student Scenes **Video** — This new video, written and acted by students from Austin, Texas, was produced in conjunction with the Texas Young Lawyers Association. Open-ended scenarios for six of the most interesting topics from the text provide rich material for discussion. Accompanying instructional materials will assist you in maximizing the benefit of this interesting videotape in your classroom.

Heart and Minds Engaged: Teaching Law-Related Education Through Service Learning **Video** — This video showing several actual service learning projects was produced by the University of Puget Sound Institute for Citizen Education in the Law. The video is an excellent resource for designing and implementing service learning in your community. Extensive teacher support materials are included.

Introduction to Law and the Legal System

Chapter 1

Vocabulary Building: Word Search 1-1

Find the following vocabulary words in the word search puzzle, and then on a separate piece of paper, write a sentence using each word you have found.

ADVERSARY	AGENCY	APPEAL
ARBITRATION	CIVIL	CRIMINAL
FEDERALISM	FELONY	INITIATIVE
JUDGE	JURISPRUDENCE	LITIGATOR
LOBBYING	MEDIATION	MISDEMEANOR
MORALITY	PARTIES	RECALL
REFERENDUM	SETTLEMENT	STATUTE
SUPREMACY	TRIAL	

```
J  F  Y  L  A  N  I  M  I  R  C  N  Q  E  K
G  A  J  N  Y  C  A  M  E  R  P  U  S  G  Z
V  D  S  E  T  T  L  E  M  E  N  T  B  D  G
Y  V  E  C  N  E  D  U  R  P  S  I  R  U  J
T  E  P  A  R  T  I  E  S  D  N  E  E  J  M
I  R  G  N  I  Y  B  B  O  L  O  T  F  W  S
L  S  T  A  T  U  T  E  D  Y  I  L  M  Y  I
A  A  T  D  I  N  I  T  I  A  T  I  V  E  L
R  R  H  M  I  S  D  E  M  E  A  N  O  R  A
O  Y  L  I  T  I  G  A  T  O  R  Y  L  E  R
M  U  D  N  E  R  E  F  E  R  T  N  A  C  E
T  S  N  L  I  V  I  C  L  X  I  O  I  A  D
M  E  D  I  A  T  I  O  N  G  B  L  R  L  E
O  V  B  Y  C  N  E  G  A  V  R  E  T  L  F
J  D  A  H  Q  L  A  E  P  P  A  F  S  K  S
```

Understanding 1-2

Write the word or phrase written in bold under its proper heading to indicate whether the word or phrase relates to checks and balances, federalism, or rights. The first one is done for you.

Congress shall make no law abridging the **freedom of speech**.

Only the U.S. Government may enter into a **treaty**.

The judicial branch can **review statutes**.

The President can **veto** Congressional acts.

Most **criminal laws** are state laws.

No citizen can be denied **equal protection**.

The government cannot impose **cruel and unusual punishment**.

States set **juror** eligibility requirements for state court.

Congress may **impeach** the President for wrongdoing.

Checks and Balances	Federalism	Rights
1. review statutes	1. _____	1. _____
2. _____	2. _____	2. _____
3. _____	3. _____	3. _____

Charting the Federal Government 1-3

Review the important government organizations below and then write them in the box under the branch of government to which they belong. For assistance, review Figure 1 in the text on page 30.

Administrative Office of the U.S. Courts

Architect of the Capitol

Congressional Budget Office

Copyright Royalty Tribunal

Council of Economic Advisors

Council on Environmental Quality

Department of Agriculture

Department of Commerce

Department of Defense

Department of Education

Department of Energy

Department of Health and
   Human Services

Department of Housing and
   Urban Development

Department of the Interior

Department of Justice

Department of Labor

Department of State

Department of Transportation

Department of the Treasury

Executive Office of the President

Federal Judicial Center

General Accounting Office

Government Printing Office

House of Representatives

Library of Congress

National Security Council

Office of Administration

Office of Management and Budget

Office of Policy Development

Office of Science and Technology Policy

Office of Technology Assessment

Office of the U.S. Trade Representative

Senate

Territorial Courts

U.S. Botanic Garden

U.S. Claims Court

U.S. Courts of Appeals

U.S. Court of Appeals for the
   Federal Circuit

U.S. Court of International Trade

U.S. Court of Military Appeals

U.S. District Courts

U.S. Tax Court

White House Office

Name_____ Date_____

Charting the Federal Government 1-3 (continued)

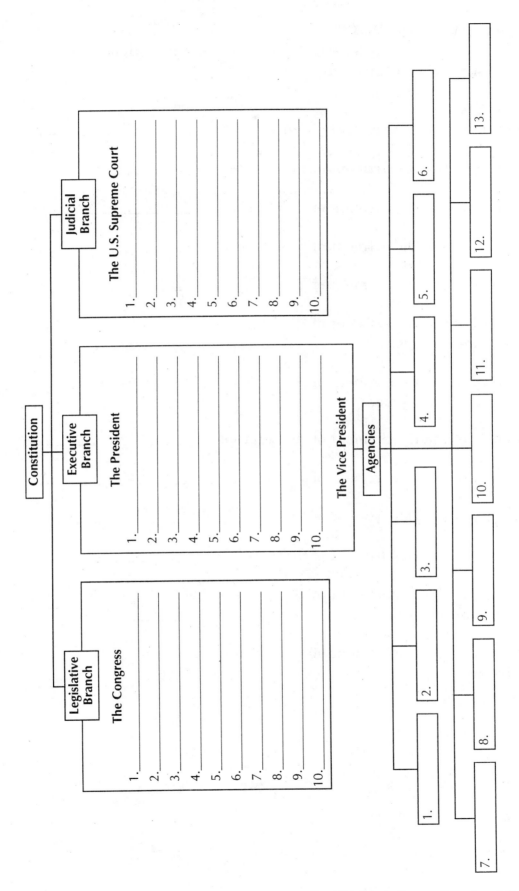

Investigating 1-4

Contact your library to determine the names of those who serve as Secretary (the head) of each of the thirteen federal agencies. List the answers in the spaces below.

Secretary of the Department of Agriculture   _____

Secretary of the Department of Commerce   _____

Secretary of the Department of Defense   _____

Secretary of the Department of Education   _____

Secretary of the Department of Energy   _____

Secretary of the Department of Health
and Human Services   _____

Secretary of the Department of Housing
and Urban Development   _____

Secretary of the Department of the Interior   _____

Secretary of the Department of Justice   _____

Secretary of the Department of Labor   _____

Secretary of the Department of State   _____

Secretary of the Department of
Transportation   _____

Secretary of the Department of
the Treasury   _____

Basic Concepts 1-5

Match each definition in the column on the left with the appropriate term in the column on the right.

1. _____ Study of law and legal philosophy

2. _____ Entitlements because a person is alive

3. _____ Crimes for which penalty is more than one year of prison

4. _____ Crimes for which penalty is one year or less

5. _____ Division of lawmaking power among three branches

6. _____ Laws made by legislatures

7. _____ The system by which each branch has the power to restrain another branch of government

8. _____ Power of courts to declare statutes void

9. _____ Provision that requires that the U.S. Constitution and federal laws are a higher authority than state laws

10. _____ The purpose for which a statute was enacted

11. _____ Authority of citizens to legislate and repeal statutes

12. _____ Actions to influence legislators

13. _____ Court decisions establishing legal principles

14. _____ Courts that hear testimony, consider evidence, and decide the facts in disputed situations

15. _____ Courts that review decisions of lower courts

16. _____ Mistakes about applicable law

17. _____ Prior case rulings that guide decisions in other cases

18. _____ Persons involved in a lawsuit

a. appeals court

b. checks and balances

c. common law

d. errors of law

e. felonies

f. human rights

g. initiatives and referendums

h. judicial review

i jurisprudence

j. legislative intent

k. lobbying

l. misdemeanors

m. parties

n. precedents

o. separation of powers

p. statutes

q. supremacy clause

r. trial courts

Name_____ Date_____

Investigating 1-6

Determine whether or not citizens of your state, county and community (town or city) have initiative and referendum power. If the answer is yes, identify a recent state initiative or referendum and present the pros and cons.

Content of Proposed Initiative or Referendum

_____

_____

_____

_____

_____

_____

_____

_____

Pros

_____

_____

_____

_____

_____

_____

_____

_____

_____

_____

Cons

_____

_____

_____

_____

_____

_____

_____

_____

_____

_____

Synthesizing 1-7

Review the types of dispute resolution in the student book on pages 42-43; 45-58: mediation, arbitration, negotiation, and litigation (the adversary system). Draw symbols that represent each of the four processes.

Negotiation

Arbitration

Mediation

Litigation

Basic Concepts 1-8

Fill in the blanks with the correct answer from the list below. Some answers may be used more than once.

defendant   lawyer

judge   plaintiff

juror   witness

jury

1.   To serve on a _____, you must be a U.S. citizen, 18 years of age, and a resident of the state.

2.   A _____ is either elected or appointed.

3.   A _____ can be removed by a peremptory challenge.

4.   A _____ presides over the trial.

5.   A _____ or a _____ decides the facts in a case.

6.   A _____ gives testimony under oath.

7.   A _____ is the person bringing a civil lawsuit.

8.   A _____ is the person being sued.

9.   A _____ is the person being charged with a crime.

10. A _____ is hired by a party or appointed by the

     _____ to represent that person.

11. A _____ is licensed by the bar association.

12. A _____ can be charged with perjury for lying under oath.

13. A _____ can be sued for malpractice.

Analyzing 1-9

Read the following case study and, on a separate sheet of paper, answer the questions which follow.

Tina, 18-years-old, had a crush on Jules, but he did not return her affection. In fact, he and his friends began to tease Tina, spitting on her and verbally abusing her. Shortly after one particularly humiliating meeting, Tina took her father's gun, went to Jules's house, and shot him to death.

Tina is not sorry for what she did because she felt insulted by Jules's actions. Tina is in jail.

1. What are the reasons for providing Tina with representation?

2. What are the reasons for not providing Tina with representation?

3. If you were a criminal defense attorney and Tina asked you to represent her, would you take her case? Why or why not?

Investigating 1-10

Investigate the following situations. Write out your findings on a separate
sheet of paper.

1. Contact your state bar association to determine what programs it offers for the
    following purposes: to help individuals find a lawyer, to handle complaints about
    a lawyer and to educate the public about the law.

2. Contact your county or local bar association to determine what programs it offers
    for the following purposes: to help individuals find a lawyer, to handle complaints
    about a lawyer and to educate the public about the law.

3. Investigate what legal services are offered to poor persons in your community.
    Determine what types of cases are handled and what the income eligibility is.

Applying the Law 1-11

Read the following hypothetical situation and answer the question which follows it.

Your father had $10,000 to invest in a business. A friend of his proposed they become partners. The friend said he had $10,000 to invest, too. Together they decided to buy a convenience store business.

Your father trusted his friend. He gave his $10,000 to him. The friend signed a receipt for the money. He now refuses to talk to your father. Your father goes to see a lawyer about helping to get back the money given to his friend.

What advice can you give your father about what he should discuss with the lawyer?

_____

_____

_____

_____

_____

_____

_____

_____

_____

_____

_____

_____

_____

_____

_____

_____

_____

_____

Ideas for Community Service Learning 1-12

- Tutor immigrants for citizenship exams.

- Help your school start a mediation program.

- Assist in cross-age teaching. Write and perform a play about the three branches of government for a younger class.

- Work on a voter registration drive or help elderly voters get to the polls on election day.

- Work at a local program which provides legal services or legal aid to the poor.

- Develop a pamphlet listing the programs in your area which provide free legal services or legal aid to the poor.

Criminal Law and Juvenile Justice

Chapter 2

Vocabulary Building: Word Search 2-1

Use the definitions to help you unscramble the vocabulary terms. Then find the vocabulary terms in the word search puzzle and circle them.

Scrambled words:

1. __ __ __ __ __ __ __ __ __. ACIRCOPSNY is the agreement between two or more persons to commit a crime.

2. __ __ __ __ __ __ __ BEBORYR is an unlawful taking of property from a person's immediate possession by force or intimidation.

3. __ __ __ __ __ __ __ __ __ __ CLCAMEPOCI is someone who helps another person commit a crime.

4. __ __ __ __ __ __ __ EAYBTRT is the unlawful physical contact inflicted by one person upon another without consent.

5. __ __ __ __ __ __ __ __ __ INPCLAPIR is the person who commits a crime.

6. __ __ __ __ __ IRCME is what one does or fails to do in violation of a law.

7. __ __ __ __ __ __ IVOEMT is the reason a person commits a crime.

8. __ __ __ __ __ __ LNYEFO is a crime for which the penalty is imprisonment for more than one year.

9. __ __ __ __ __ __ __ __ __ __ __ __ LTNICTOSOAII is crime of asking, commanding, urging or advising another person to commit a crime.

10. __ __ __ __ __ __ __ __ MCIHEDIO is the killing of a human being.

11. __ __ __ __ __ __ MCVITI is a person who is injured by the crime of another.

12. __ __ __ __ __ __ __ METTPAT is the intent to commit a crime coupled with a substantial step toward committing a crime.

13. __ __ __ __ __ __ __ __ MNEELTSE are the conditions that make an act a crime.

Vocabulary Building: Word Search 2-1 (continued)

14. __ __ __ __ __ __ __ __ __ __ __ NDSMAIREEMO is any crime for which the penalty is one year or less.

15. __ __ __ __ __ __ NTTIEN is the mental state that a person intended or meant to commit a crime.

16. __ __ __ __ __ RASON is the willful and malicious burning of another's property.

17. __ __ __ __ __ __ __ __ __ SADLIMNAV is the willful destruction of, or damage to, the property of another.

18. __ __ __ __ __ __ __ SEDNEEF is the legal or factual excuse to crime.

19. __ __ __ __ __ __ __ __ __ __ UHINTESAAA is the act or method of putting someone to death painlessly to end suffering.

20. __ __ __ __ __ __ __ __ __ __ __ UITTSOTRNIE is requiring criminals to pay back or otherwise compensate the victims of their crime.

```
B  K  N  I  Y  C  A  R  I  P  S  N  O  C  L
Z  H  O  W  L  V  K  L  D  T  B  N  H  K  A
O  Z  I  N  T  E  N  T  N  A  O  O  N  R  P
D  V  T  H  O  Z  J  E  T  B  M  Q  O  A  I
T  M  A  A  M  X  M  T  S  I  C  N  R  I  C
F  S  T  N  E  E  M  C  B  A  S  H  S  N
E  I  I  T  L  R  Y  I  K  E  O  T  L  A  I
L  L  C  E  Y  V  D  R  M  N  U  D  T  N  R
O  A  I  M  T  E  E  E  E  O  Q  D  F  A  P
N  D  L  P  R  C  D  M  F  B  T  J  T  H  C
Y  N  O  T  V  S  O  R  I  E  B  I  E  T  K
I  A  S  Z  I  E  A  J  E  R  N  O  V  U  C
U  V  M  M  I  T  C  I  V  U  C  S  R  E  I
N  O  I  T  U  T  I  T  S  E  R  Q  E  R  A
E  C  I  L  P  M  O  C  C  A  Q  F  B  T  A
```

Basic Concepts 2-2
Write the term from the list below next to the appropriate definition.

arson	larceny
assault	negligent homicide
auto theft	receiving stolen property
battery	robbery
burglary	second degree murder
computer crime	sexual assault
copyright violation	shoplifting
date or acquaintance rape	statutory rape
driving while intoxicated	suicide
embezzlement	tobacco sales to minors
extortion	unauthorized use of a vehicle
felony murder	uttering
first degree murder	vandalism
forgery	voluntary manslaughter
involuntary manslaughter	

1. Offering to someone as genuine a document known to be a fake

   _____

2. Killing done with malice but without premeditation

   _____

3. Deliberate taking of one's own life

   _____

4. Sales of cigarettes and related products to persons under 18 years of age

   _____

Basic Concepts 2-2 (continued)

5. Killing that is premeditated, deliberate and done with malice

_____

6. Falsely making or altering a writing or document with intent to defraud

_____

7. Unauthorized access, use, alteration, or taking of another person's computer systems or files

_____

8. Unlawful taking of property from a person's immediate possession by force or intimidation

_____

9. Receiving property from another person whom that person knows, or has reason to know, is not legally in control of the property

_____

10. Illegal copying of computer software

_____

11. Unauthorized taking of a vehicle temporarily

_____

12. Sexual assault by someone known to the victim

_____

13. Using threats to obtain the property of another

_____

Basic Concepts 2-2 (continued)

14. Willful destruction of, or damage to, the property of another

_____

15. Killing as part of the commission of certain serious crimes

_____

16. Operating a car while affected by alcohol

_____

17. Unauthorized entry into any structure with the intent to commit a crime

_____

18. Killing as a result of the failure to use reasonable care

_____

19. Unlawful taking of property by someone to whom it was entrusted

_____

20. Taking items from a store without paying or intending to pay for them

_____

21. Sexual intercourse committed by force and without consent

_____

22. Unlawful taking and carrying away of the property of another with intent to steal it

_____

Basic Concepts 2-2 (continued)

23. Unauthorized taking of a vehicle without the intent to return it

_____

24. Attempting or threatening to carry out a physical attack upon another person

_____

25. Sexual intercourse with an underage person whether or not there is consent

_____

26. Killing under circumstances that lessen but do not excuse the killing

_____

27. Willful and malicious burning of another's property

_____

28. Unlawful physical contact inflicted by one person upon another without consent

_____

29. Unintentional killing from extremely reckless conduct

_____

Understanding 2-3

Review these property crimes defined in the text on pages 94-101. Then draw a picture for each crime to demonstrate the differences among these crimes.

Robbery   **Vandalism**

Larceny   **Embezzlement**

Burglary   **Forgery**

Analyzing 2-4

Read through the following case study and opinions one and two. Answer the questions that follow.

An African-American police officer saw three young African-American men walking at 8 p.m. in a mainly Caucasian suburb. One of them carried a duffel bag. Another was carrying a brown paper bag. The third, Darron Barber, was carrying a bundle wrapped in a multi-colored blanket. The bags appeared to be filled with objects of some kind.

After the officer had driven past, he continued to observe the three through his rear-view mirror. The three continued to glance at him and at each other. Through his mirror, the officer observed the male who was carrying the blanketed bundle throw it off the shoulder of the roadway. The contents seemed to be very heavy because they did not get thrown far.

The officer made a U-turn, drove back, stopped and began questioning the three men. He patted each down for weapons and found none. He then advised each man of his Miranda warnings. The officer did not believe the three men were under arrest at that time.

Two of the men put what they were carrying, the duffel bag and brown paper bag, on the ground. The paper bag was open and the officer observed two telephones and two cartons of Kool cigarettes. Mr. Barber stated he did not want to answer any questions and made movements as if he was going to leave the scene. Officer Hershey then handcuffed the Mr. Barber to keep him at the scene.

The police officer separated the men and asked them questions. The young men gave different answers about what they were doing. Mr. Barber also denied having thrown anything in the bushes.

The officer patted down the duffel bag for weapons and recognized the contents as electronic equipment. Other officers arrived and one retrieved a videocassette recorder. Another officer with a tracking dog followed the scent to an apartment. The officer reported on the radio that a recent burglary had been committed. A Hitachi VCR, telephones, and a multicolored afghan had been stolen. After confirming that the VCR found in the brush was the same make, the officers arrested the three men. The initial stop to the arrest took 15 minutes.

Analyzing 2-4 (continued)

Opinion one

The officer's initial stop of the three males was not based on a well-founded suspicion of criminal activity based upon specific facts. Instead, the officer made the stop of the three men solely because they were African-American individuals in a predominantly Caucasian neighborhood. The officer would not have slowed down to look at the men twice had they not been African American. The fact that the officer is African American does not make the stop any more acceptable. The officer's hunch that the men had violated the law turned out to be correct. However, this fact does not make the stop any more acceptable.

The stop was thus illegal, and all the evidence gathered as a result of this illegal stop cannot be used in a criminal prosecution.

Opinion two

The officer's initial stop of the three males was based on a well-founded suspicion of criminal activity based upon specific facts. The officer stopped the men because one of the three was carrying a large blanket-covered bundle.

As the officer drove past, he continued observing them and they continued to glance at him and at each other. The officer saw the one carrying the blanketed bundle throw what appeared to be a very heavy bundle into the brush. This amounted at least to littering.

With ten years' experience behind him, the officer recognized that when a person carries a bundle under a blanket on a street at night, the hidden items are usually from a recent burglary.

The men were walking in the street in violation of the law.

The officer's detention of the three men was reasonably related to the stop. The purpose of the stop was related to the men's subsequent detention. The amount of intrusion upon the men in the course of the detention was reasonable, and the length of the men's detention was reasonable.

Opening and viewing the contents of the duffel bag was lawful. When he originally patted down the duffel bag for weapons, the officer inadvertently discovered that the bag contained electronic equipment. After reviewing the radio report from the officer with the tracking dog what items had been burglarized, the officer involved in the stop had every reason to believe the duffel bag contained contraband from the burglary. The stop and the search were legal.

Analyzing 2-4 (continued)

1. Identify and write out the arguments in opinion one.

_____

_____

_____

_____

_____

_____

_____

_____

_____

_____

2. Identify and write out the arguments in opinion two.

_____

_____

_____

_____

_____

_____

_____

_____

_____

_____

_____

Analyzing 2-4 (continued)

3. Which opinion do you agree with? State why.

_____

_____

_____

_____

_____

_____

_____

_____

_____

_____

_____

_____

_____

_____

_____

_____

_____

_____

Graphs 2-5

Review the chart of crimes reported on page 62 of the text. Translate the information on the total number of reported crimes to this bar graph. For each bar write in the correct crime from the list below. The first one is done for you.

murder and non-negligent manslaughter

forcible rape

robbery

aggravated assault

burglary

larceny/theft

motor vehicle theft

arson

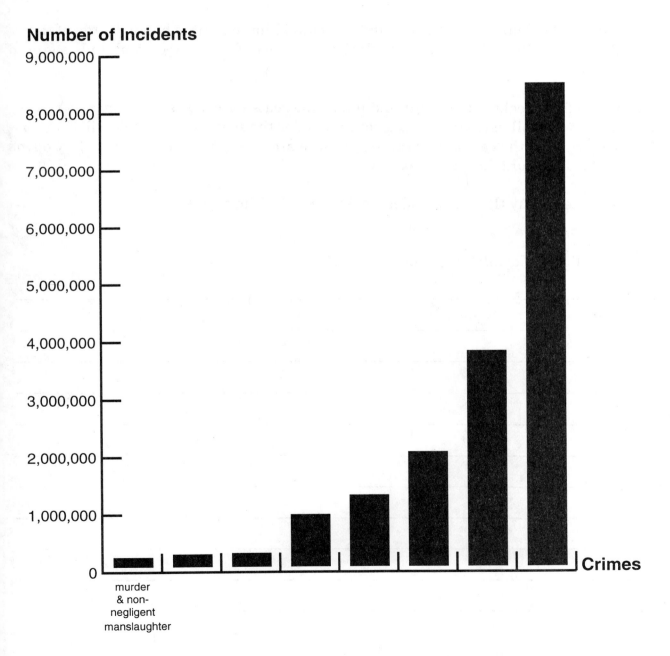

Number of Incidents

Applying Knowledge 2-6

Review the rules in the text on arrests on pages 114-120. Read through the following case study and then answer the question that follows.

Thuy is 20 years old and does not speak much English. He is a gang member. He is driving a new car that he bought with drug money. Thuy is wearing all black clothing.

Two police officers in a police car stop Thuy because they think that he might be a gang member who sells drugs. They think this because he is a young Asian male, he is driving a new car and he is wearing all black.

The police order Thuy out of the car and command him to put his hands on top of the car. One police officer pats down Thuy's clothing to feel for a weapon and finds a gun in Thuy's pants.

The other officer looks into the car and under the seats for drugs and weapons. The officer finds a small package of crack cocaine under the seat. The officers tell Thuy to open the trunk of the car so they can see if there are more drugs in the car. Thuy opens the trunk. The trunk has more cocaine.

The police tell Thuy that he is under arrest and take him to jail.

Did the police act legally? Why, or why not?

_____

_____

_____

_____

_____

_____

_____

_____

_____

_____

Basic Concepts 2-7

Fill in the blanks with the proper word or words from the list below. Words may be used more than once.

accused	offense
armed	personal appearance
arrest	probable cause
arrest warrant	reasonably necessary
belief	stop and frisk
crime	victim
drug courier profiles	witness
force	

1. An _____ means that a person suspected of a crime is taken into custody.

2. An _____ is a court order commanding that the person named be taken into custody.

3. The person filing a complaint for an arrest warrant may be a _____, a _____ or a _____.

4. Based on the information provided, the judge must find _____ to believe that an _____ has been committed and that the _____ committed it in order to issue an arrest warrant.

5. _____ is defined as a reasonable _____ that a person has committed a _____.

6. Police may use _____ to help establish _____ to arrest, which is based on commonly held notions concerning a persons' age, race, _____, and mannerisms.

7. Officers who think a person is behaving suspiciously and is likely to be _____, may _____ the suspect for _____.

8. A police officer may use as much physical _____ as is _____ to make an _____.

Criminal Law and Juvenile Justice

Analyzing 2-8

Read through the following case study and then answer the question that follows.

Rodney was injured in a motorcycle accident. When the paramedic arrived, he found Rodney unconscious and lying face down on the street. To see how badly Rodney was hurt, the paramedic cut away his clothes and rolled him on his back. A pouch containing $11,000 was found on his stomach. In accordance with his training, the paramedic searched Rodney's clothing for valuables, to protect himself from later accusations that he may have stolen something from the injured man.

In Rodney's pants, the paramedic found a knife, a notebook and a small plastic container, later discovered to contain heroin. The paramedic turned the money and drugs over to the police officer at the scene.

Were Rodney's Fourth Amendment rights violated? Give reasons for your answer.

_____

_____

_____

_____

_____

_____

_____

_____

_____

_____

_____

_____

_____

Analyzing and Investigating 2-9

Identify the procedure in your community for making complaints about police conduct. Find out how many complaints have been made in the past year, what government body handles the complaints, who makes up that government body, and what the outcomes of the complaints have been. Write your findings below.

_____

_____

_____

_____

_____

_____

_____

_____

_____

_____

_____

_____

_____

_____

_____

_____

_____

_____

_____

_____

_____

Writing 2-10

Assume that the incident below happened to you. On a separate sheet of paper, write a letter of complaint about the incident to the chief of police.

You are driving home at about 10 p.m. on Saturday, February 5, from your job in a local store. It is dark and raining very hard. You come to a stop sign on Cherry Street at the intersection with 16th St. You slow down, but then ease through the intersection without coming to a complete stop.

A police car turns on the lights behind you and you pull over. The officer asks to see your driver's license. You ask what you have done wrong, but the officer refuses to tell you. You notice the officer's badge number is 2056, that the officer is tall, has brown hair and has a mole under the right eye.

The officer shines a light on your face and then asks you to get into the police car and go to have some coffee at a nearby cafe. The officer promises to overlook your illegal activity if you come along. You refuse. The officer shouts at you to get out of the area. You go home feeling angry and that your rights have been violated.

Name_____ Date_____

Understanding 2-11

Read through the list of procedures. Next to each procedure circle all the persons who are involved in that procedure. Some procedures involve more than one person.

Procedures: Involved Persons:

1. arraignment   accused   corrections officials   defense attorney
                         jail official   judge   jury   police   prosecutor

2. arrest   accused   corrections officials   defense attorney
                         jail official   judge   jury   police   prosecutor

3. booking   accused   corrections officials   defense attorney
                         jail official   judge   jury   police   prosecutor

4. fingerprinting   accused   corrections officials   defense attorney
    & photographing   jail official   judge   jury   police   prosecutor

5. imprisonment   accused   corrections officials   defense attorney
                         jail official   judge   jury   police   prosecutor

6. initial appearance   accused   corrections officials   defense attorney
                         jail official   judge   jury   police   prosecutor

7. plea bargaining   accused   corrections officials   defense attorney
                         jail official   judge   jury   police   prosecutor

8. pretrial motions   accused   corrections officials   defense attorney
                         jail official   judge   jury   police   prosecutor

9. pretrial release   accused   corrections officials   defense attorney
                         jail official   judge   jury   police   prosecutor

Understanding 2-11 (continued)

10. sentencing   accused   corrections officials   defense attorney
                             jail official   judge   jury   police   prosecutor

11. trial   accused   corrections officials   defense attorney
                             jail official   judge   jury   police   prosecutor

12. verdict   accused   corrections officials   defense attorney
                             jail official   judge   jury   police   prosecutor

Graphs 2-12

Review the graph on pages 158 in the student text. Determine for each of the lines in the graph below what is represented. The first one is done for you.

fines

probation

total convicted

total defendants

total imprisoned

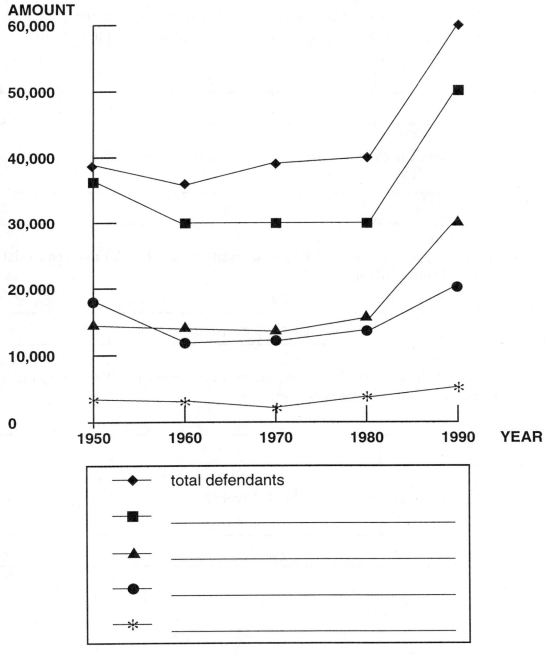

Expressing Your Opinion With Reasons 2-13

Imagine that you are in charge of revising the juvenile justice system for your state. In designing the best system, consider the following features. Check those that you would include. Give your reasons.

1. _____ My system will have a mediation program for the victim and the juvenile offender.

   Reasons: _____

   _____

2. _____ My system will have a "three strikes, you're out" requirement; juveniles committing three serious felonies will be treated as adults and locked up for life.

   Reasons: _____

   _____

3. _____ My system will provide boot camp experiences for offenders.

   Reasons: _____

   _____

4. _____ My juvenile justice system will put parents in jail for offenses committed by their minor children.

   Reasons: _____

   _____

5. _____ My system will have a heavy emphasis on imprisonment to hold youth accountable for their offenses.

   Reasons: _____

   _____

6. _____ My system will provide juries in all juvenile cases.

   Reasons: _____

   _____

Expressing Your Opinion With Reasons 2-13 (continued)

7. _____ My system will allow judges to be free to decide which sentence best fits each individual, taking into account the circumstances of each offender.

Reasons: _____

_____

8. _____ In my system, there will not be a separate juvenile justice system; all offenders will go to the same court.

Reasons: _____

_____

9. _____ My system will feature alternatives to detention.

Reasons: _____

_____

10. _____ In my system, juveniles may be punished by caning (corporal punishment).

Reasons: _____

_____

Ideas for Community Service Learning 2-14

- Start a school crime watch.

- Start a neighborhood crime watch.

- Get involved in crime prevention education for peers, younger students, neighbors, or the elderly.

- Present a mock trial of a criminal law issue for younger students.

- Start an anti-graffiti campaign.

- Assist juveniles returning from the juvenile justice system to stay in school.

TORTS

Chapter 3

Vocabulary Building: Word Scramble 3-1

Use the definitions to help you unscramble the vocabulary terms.

Scrambled words:

1. __ __ __ __ __ __ __ ASATSLU is the threat of immediate harm from battery.

2. __ __ __ __ __ __ __ __ __ BIIYLTIAL is the legal responsibility for an injury.

3. __ __ __ __ __ __ __ CTNNSEO is a defense to battery.

4. __ __ __ __ __ __ DRYEEM is an action to make up for injury.

5. __ __ __ __ __ __ __ EASAMDG are the payment of money to make up for injuries.

6. __ __ __ __ __ __ __ __ __ __ ICMPTARECLA is the lack of reasonable care by a professional.

7. __ __ __ __ __ __ __ __ __ ILEVGRPEI is a public policy that permits the defendant to act.

8. __ __ __ __ __ __ __ __ __ __ IONRNSEOCV is the unlawful exercise of control over another's personal property.

9. __ __ __ __ __ __ __ __ __ __ LTDUDCIBEE is the amount an insured is required to pay before insurance pays.

10. __ __ __ __ __ __ __ __ __ __ __ __ LUTMNOACREIC is a defendant's action against the plaintiff.

11. __ __ __ __ __ __ MUNEIM means a person is protected from some kinds of tort suits.

12. __ __ __ __ __ __ __ __ NEACUISN is an unreasonable interference with property.

13. __ __ __ __ __ __ __ __ __ __ NEGCNILGEE is the failure to use reasonable care, which causes harm.

Vocabulary Building: Word Scramble 3-1 (continued)

14. ___ ___ ___ ___ ___ ___ ___ ___ ___ NESRANCIU is a purchased plan to pay for losses.

15. ___ ___ ___ ___ ___ ___ ___ NFEDESE is a legal excuse to torts.

16. ___ ___ ___ ___ ___ ___ ___ ___ ___ PNATFFIIL is the injured party in a tort suit.

17. ___ ___ ___ ___ ___ ___ ___ ___ PUIMERSM are insurance payments.

18. ___ ___ ___ ___ ___ ___ ___ ___ RSAPETSS is entering property without permission.

19. ___ ___ ___ ___ ___ ___ ___ ___ ___ TMEEESTLNT is an agreement to resolve a dispute.

20. ___ ___ ___ ___ ___ ___ ___ ___ ___ TNDOIEIAM is a process in which a third person assists people with settling a dispute without going to court.

21. ___ ___ ___ ___ ___ ___ ___ ___ ___ ___ TNIUCIJNNO is a court order to do or not to do something.

22. ___ ___ ___ ___ ___ ___ ___ YETTRBA is an intentional act to cause harmful contact of another person.

Analyzing 3-2

Read the case that follows keeping strict liability in mind. On a separate piece of paper, decide the case. Give your reasons.

Vasily hated opening the hot-dog stand for the summer season. There was always so much to do — cleaning, painting, stocking. It never seemed to stop. But, as much as he hated it, he liked making the money that kept his car on the road. The boss had asked him to make sure that the rest rooms were clean so that employees could use them.

The toilet bowl looked pretty bad. Water dripping all winter had left a lot of rust. This was going to be a tough one. As soon as Vasily dumped the cleaner in the bowl a cloud of gas escaped, choking him. His boss heard Vasily choking and rushed him to the hospital. He was treated at the hospital for 122 days for acute bronchitis and acute asthma.

His lungs were permanently damaged. Participating in sports was out of the question. He could hardly breathe and it wasn't going to improve.

Vasily sued the manufacturer of the cleaner for his injuries. Experts testified that sodium bisulfate and a chlorine ion in the bowl cleaner would react with iron oxide to release poisonous chlorine and hydrogen chloride gases. Vasily testified that he did not know what chemicals had caused his injury. There was no warning label. The manufacturer contended that there was no direct proof that the cleaner had, in fact, caused Vasily's injury.

Analyzing 3-3

Read the case that follows keeping strict liability in mind. On a separate piece of paper, decide the case. Give your reasons.

Kai-Lin's boss wanted to display some new items in the store. He asked Kai-Lin to use some polyurethane foam sheets to make a little display box and gave Kai-Lin a soldering gun to melt the foam and cut it into pieces that were the size she needed to make the box.

During heating the foam gave off smoke and fumes. Shortly thereafter, Kai-Lin was diagnosed as having a progressive, debilitating illness that caused shortness of breath, reduced pulmonary function, bronchitis and chest pains. She sued the manufacturer of the foam. Experts testified that such illness may be caused by toluene diisocyanate (TDI), a chemical used to make polyurethane that remains in the foam.

OSHA has found it to be dangerous in concentrations above 0.02 parts per million for 20 minutes. Kai-Lin testified that she was never warned of any hazard in heating the material and that she didn't see a warning label that was included with each shipment.

She argued that each sheet should have had the label stapled to it so that the ultimate user could not avoid seeing it. Her lawyers did not indicate that the warning sheet itself was inadequate, only that its distribution was faulty.

The manufacturer countered that the employer had received a 40-page safety booklet that experts testified was one of the best in the industry, that the employer also had had personal experience that indicated that these materials were hazardous under certain conditions, and that stapling the safety note to the sheets would have destroyed the sheets and many of the notes would have been torn off during packaging. In addition, the company only sold the materials to knowledgeable customers, gave them clear warning of the dangers inherent in using the product including cutting it with a hot wire or heat contact. They indicated that this process should only be done with adequate ventilation.

Understanding 3-4

Read through the following terms and decide which are torts and which are defenses to torts. Write the name of each tort inside the ovals, and then write the defenses that apply to that tort in the rectangles surrounding the ovals. The first one is done for you.

assumption of the risk
battery
comparative negligence
consent
contributory negligence
defamation
lack of malice
misuse of product by consumer
negligence
opinion
self-defense
strict liability acts
truth

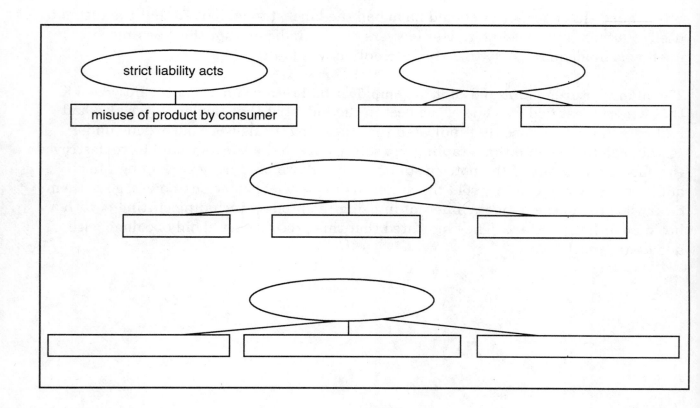

Basic Concepts 3-5

Write **T** for True, or **F** for False next to each of the statements. If the statement is false, rewrite the sentence on a separate sheet of paper to make it true.

1. _____ Tort law deals with society's right to punish people who have disobeyed the law.

2. _____ Few activities can be the source of tort liability.

3. _____ Damages are a form of remedy available in tort suits.

4. _____ All injuries caused by others result in compensation.

5. _____ All people are required to act with reasonable care toward other people and their property.

6. _____ The definition of what is reasonable is difficult to determine.

7. _____ Agreement between two parties on how to remedy an injury is called liability.

8. _____ 90% of tort cases filed in court go to trial.

9. _____ Tort liability exists for three major categories of conduct: intentional wrongs, negligence and crimes.

10. _____ The law grants immunity to children so that they cannot be sued for their torts.

11. _____ Contingency fees require the client to pay the lawyer an hourly rate.

12. _____ Class actions are tort suits with many plaintiffs.

Basic Concepts 3-6
Fill in the blanks with the correct answer from the list below.

accidents   limits
collision coverage   malpractice insurance
comprehensive coverage   mediation
contract   medical insurance
damages   negotiation
homeowner's insurance   other people
insured person   premiums
insurance company   property
lawsuit   representation

1. A victim of a tort should always consider _____
   or _____, before filing a _____.

2. Liability insurance is a _____ between the
   _____ and the _____.

3. The insurance company promises to pay for _____ and the
   insured person promises to pay _____.

4. _____ covers professionals for their negligent actions.

5. A person whose home is destroyed by fire may be able to recover the cost of the
   house through _____.

6. Liability insurance pays for injuries to _____ and
   _____, and may also include _____.

7. _____ pays for damage to the insured person's car even if the
   insured person caused the accident.

8. Insurance has _____ which set the top amount the insurance
   company will pay.

9. _____ pays for the insured person's medical expenses resulting
   from _____ involving the insured person's car or the car the
   insured person is driving.

10. If someone writes graffiti all over the car and now the car must be repainted at a
    cost of $500, the car owner can have this paid by the insurance company if they
    have _____.

Investigating 3-7

Determine whether your state has a fault or no-fault insurance system. If it is a no-fault system, determine what is the maximum amount that will be paid. Find out whether or not all drivers must have insurance and the penalty for failing to have insurance. Is there a minimum amount of insurance that must be carried?

Write your findings below.

_____

_____

_____

_____

_____

_____

_____

_____

_____

_____

_____

_____

_____

_____

_____

_____

_____

_____

_____

_____

Name_____ Date_____

Ideas for Community Service Learning 3-8

- Write and produce a play or video about negligence to be viewed by younger students. For example a comedy could be written illustrating the "reasonable person standard."

- Write and distribute an informational pamphlet for high school students about car insurance. The pamphlet should include what to do if you are involved in a car accident.

Consumer Law

Chapter 4

Vocabulary Building: Word Search 4-1

Review the vocabulary terms in the Consumer Law Chapter to help you
unscramble the words below. Then find the vocabulary terms in the word
search puzzle and circle them. Finally, on a separate sheet of paper, write
a sentence using each vocabulary term.

Scrambled words:

1. ANOTTCCR   __ __ __ __ __ __ __ __

2. AURFD   __ __ __ __ __

3. DLSIIMCAER   __ __ __ __ __ __ __ __ __

4. EDBSRTO   __ __ __ __ __ __ __

5. ENATCAPCCE   __ __ __ __ __ __ __ __ __ __

6. ENTSRGHMAIN   __ __ __ __ __ __ __ __ __ __ __

7. IOSICSSERN   __ __ __ __ __ __ __ __ __ __

8. IUFPGNF   __ __ __ __ __ __ __

9. LUAFDTE   __ __ __ __ __ __ __

10. NESOMURC   __ __ __ __ __ __ __ __

11. NETTACAHTM   __ __ __ __ __ __ __ __ __ __

12. NTISERET   __ __ __ __ __ __ __ __

13. OFERF   __ __ __ __ __

14. OSCING   __ __ __ __ __ __

Vocabulary Building: Word Search 4-1 (continued)

15. RECHBDEA   __ __ __ __ __ __ __ __

16. RRWANTAY   __ __ __ __ __ __ __ __

17. SMAAGDE   __ __ __ __ __ __ __

18. TRIOCRSDE   __ __ __ __ __ __ __ __ __

19. TSOTUIRITEN   __ __ __ __ __ __ __ __ __ __ __

```
T   E   C   N   A   T   P   E   C   C   A   Z   U   A   P
N   D   A   T   T   A   C   H   M   E   N   T   N   O   P
E   I   E   N   X   F   R   M   G   N   I   F   F   U   P
M   D   S   H   O   V   C   H   Y   F   G   R   N   D   S
H   E   U   L   C   I   U   E   S   A   I   A   O   M   Y
S   B   S   D   A   A   T   K   Z   R   E   U   I   S   T
I   T   Q   F   O   R   E   U   Q   E   H   D   S   E   N
N   O   F   F   E   R   E   R   T   M   V   X   S   G   A
R   R   Q   P   O   B   Q   T   B   I   R   Y   I   A   R
A   S   S   K   J   Y   Y   K   A   A   T   S   C   M   R
G   T   S   E   R   E   T   N   I   L   O   S   S   A   A
W   C   O   N   S   U   M   E   R   C   L   I   E   D   W
D   C   R   E   D   I   T   O   R   S   I   O   R   R   X
T   C   A   R   T   N   O   C   G   I   I   A   C   S   F
Z   H   K   T   L   U   A   F   E   D   N   W   D   W   J
```

Basic Concepts 4-2

Determine whether each statement is true or false. Write **T** for True, or **F** for False next to each of the statements.

1. _____ It is generally a good idea to buy expensive items the first time that you see them advertised on sale.

2. _____ Comparison shopping means that you examine all the items in the store where you bought the item to make sure that you got the best one.

3. _____ If you buy an item without signing a contract, then there is no contract.

4. _____ The Better Business Bureau may be able to give information about businesses which are not members of the Better Business Bureau.

5. _____ If you are making a major purchase and the seller hands you a detailed contract which you do not understand, you should ask to take the contract to someone who can help you understand it before you sign it.

6. _____ The first thing you should do after buying a product is to inspect it.

7. _____ If you and the seller go to binding arbitration, you can still go to court if you do not like the outcome.

8. _____ Mediation is a process in which another person helps the buyer and seller find an acceptable solution to their problem.

9. _____ A buyer asks a court to award damages when the buyer wants the court to cancel a contract.

10. _____ A buyer asks a court to order specific performance when the buyer wants the court to order the seller to carry out the specific terms of the agreement.

11. _____ Most consumer cases go to criminal court.

12. _____ Attorneys are required in small claims court.

Applying Knowledge 4-3

Identify which federal act covers the following consumer problems.

Federal Trade Commission Act

Consumer Product Safety Act

Nutrition Labeling and Education Act

Americans with Disabilities Act

1. SlimDown Company has developed a new weight loss drink. The label claims that users will lose 5 pounds per week by drinking one can per day. Users are free to eat as much as they wish of any other foods. People using the drink do not lose weight.

   _____

2. Ace Furnace Company sends out representatives door to door. They tell the home owners that they will do a free inspection of the furnace for safety and upkeep problems. After the furnace is inspected, which requires taking it apart, the representative refuses to put the furnace back together until the individual signs a service contract.

   _____

3. Maria has cerebral palsy and is confined to a wheelchair. She is denied entrance to a restaurant because the manager says that the customers do not want to have to look at her.

   _____

4. The Good Earth Company advertises on its label that its new margarine is low in sodium and low in fat. In fact, the margarine has the same fat content as butter.

   _____

5. Kim bought a food processor. During the first week she used it, the cutting blade broke off. While she was returning the food processor to the store, another person came in to the store to return his food processor. The cutting blade had broken off his during machine the second week of use. Each of them got a refund.

   _____

Investigating 4-4

Which goods or services do you think consumers in your state complain about the most? Investigate by contacting the local chapter of the Better Business Bureau, the State's Attorney General's Office, a consumer protection agency or the local person who handles consumer affairs with the media.

Make a written comparison of your results. Include a list of the top ten goods or services that consumers have complained about in your state. Write your findings on a separate sheet of paper. Be sure to include where you got your information. Does your list have any of the same items as the list below?

1. New and used motor vehicle sales

2. Retail operations

3. Motor vehicle repairs

4. Direct mail advertising

5. Contractors

6. Health clubs

7. Credit

8. Telemarketing

9. Catalog/mail order

10. Books/magazines

Name_____ Date_____

Analyzing and Investigating 4-5

Identify a major purchase that you would like to make or have recently made (a CD player, car, etc.) and use *Consumer Reports,* or some other book or magazine which rates products, to find out how your purchase is rated. Report below what you found out.

_____

_____

_____

_____

_____

_____

_____

_____

_____

_____

_____

_____

_____

_____

_____

_____

_____

_____

_____

_____

_____

Consumer Law

Writing 4-6

Review the tips on writing a consumer letter of complaint found on pages 262-263 of the text. Draft a letter to Helen, the owner of Leather Outfitters, using the tips.

You went on vacation in another state. As a special treat for yourself, you bought a leather backpack that was decorated with metal ornaments. You bought the backpack from Helen, the owner of Leather Outfitters for $79 on July 28.

On August 3, as you were traveling back home, one of the metal decorations broke off. You called Helen at Leather Outfitters from the phone number listed on the receipt that you kept. Helen told you that she was sorry but that all sales are final.

You took the backpack to a leather repair shop. The owner told you that the backpack could not be fixed.

_____

_____

_____

_____

_____

_____

_____

_____

_____

_____

_____

_____

_____

_____

_____

_____

Basic Concepts 4-7

Write the word or phrase from the list below under the appropriate description.

association approach

bait and switch

bandwagon approach

claims of authorities' approach

cooling-off period

corrective advertising

deceptive advertising

lien

loss leaders

open-ended estimate

puffing

1. For six months, manufacturers of Splash mouth wash must include in its advertisements that it had falsely claimed in prior ads that its product killed bacteria.

   _____

2. Minh signed a contract for a home security system that she bought from a man who came to her house. Two days later, she decided to cancel the contract.

   _____

3. Murray bought a time-share apartment after reading an ad in the newspaper that the apartment was built on a beautiful lake. When Murray visited the apartment, he discovered that the lake was all dried up.

   _____

4. The saleswoman told La Verne that the shoes she was considering buying were the best in the world.

   _____

5. An ad for lipstick says, "Go red, everybody else is!"

   _____

Basic Concepts 4-7 (continued)

6. An ad for milk shows a mother feeding her baby.

   _____

7. An ad for headache medicine states that more doctors and hospitals use their product than any other headache medicine.

   _____

8. After advertising its washing machine for $99, the seller tells each customer that the washer does not get clothes white and clean. The seller also tells the customers that only one $99 washing machine is left, and then he directs them to a $400 washing machine.

   _____

9. Virgil answers an advertisement offering 35 mm cameras for $20. The camera salesperson demonstrates the $20 camera and also tells him that although they have plenty of these cameras in stock, they have more expensive camera with greater accuracy available.

   _____

10. Jane brought her car to a mechanic. Al estimated that the repairs would cost $125 and asked Jane to sign the estimate. She also was asked to sign an agreement that allowed Al to make all repairs that Al deemed were necessary.

   _____

11. Jim had his car repaired at Al's. Jim did not pay his bill. Al kept his car and would not release it until Jim paid.

   _____

Expressing Your Opinion 4-8

Read the following cases and decide whether or not the merchant's actions are legal or illegal. Write **L** for Legal and **I** for Illegal next to each of the statements, and then write your reasons for your answers. If you think you need more information, put **U** for Undecided, and list what information is needed.

1. _____ Tyrone and Angelique see an ad for "freight damaged dining room tables on sale for $300." They go to the store where Al explains that the damaged tables have been sold. However, they do have dining room tables for $600 in stock.

   Reasons:_____

   _____

   _____

2. _____ When Tyrone and Angelique arrive at the store to buy this freight-damaged table, Al shows them the table for $300. He also suggests that a much nicer one is available for $600.

   Reasons:_____

   _____

   _____

3. _____ Cheetham's Sales offers a free one-carat emerald to anyone who comes to their one-hour presentation on condominiums. Sean goes to the presentation and is subjected to high-pressure sales tactics to buy a condominium. He resists and leaves with a low quality one-carat emerald worth $2.00.

   Reasons:_____

   _____

   _____

Expressing Your Opinion 4-8 (continued)

4. _____ A New Age Encyclopedia representative comes to T.D.'s home and interviews him about his beliefs in education. As a result of T.D.'s answers, New Age says he has won a contest and they will place an encyclopedia in his home at no cost. T.D.'s only obligation is to pay for annual supplements at $50 each for the next ten years. T.D. must pay for these ten supplements ($500) in advance.

   Reasons:_____

   _____

   _____

5. _____ Mohammed goes to a beef outlet store after seeing an ad for beef at a low price. He orders 100 lbs. of beef and the meat dealer asks, "Do you use a lot of fat? You don't by any chance make your own soap, do you?" Mohammed says no and the dealer then encourages him to buy better quality, more expensive meat.

   Reasons:_____

   _____

   _____

6. _____ Rachel receives a postcard offering her a "thrilling, heart-shaped 14-karat gold-flash medallion containing 10,000 dazzling diamonds and one matching 14-karat gold-flash 18-inch necklace" from Henri Hamilton of J.E.N. Jewels of New York. The cost is just $3.00. She calls the 900 number on the post-card and is told all of the advertised necklaces are gone. Later, her phone bill includes a charge of $6.95 for the 900 number call.

   Reasons:_____

   _____

   _____

Analyzing 4-9

Read the following telephone conversation and answer the questions that follow.

Narrator: "Romel, an 18-year old high school student, was home one night watching his favorite TV show, when the phone rang. The following conversation took place:"

Caller: "Is this Romel Martinez?"

Romel: "Yes, it is."

Caller: "Romel, this is Diana at Acme Tel-Sale Company. How are you this evening?"

Romel: "I'm okay, but I'm in the middle of watching my favorite TV show."

Caller: "Don't worry, this will only take a minute of your valuable time. I have an exceptional offer for you. Did you receive our postcard this week?"

Romel: "Uhh, I'm not sure."

Caller: "You have been selected as one of a very few customers to participate in our exclusive marketing survey. You will receive as a gift from Acme, absolutely free, either a freshwater fishing boat or a motorcycle if you will simply agree to test one of these products for us. As your postcard stated, however, this offer expires at midnight tonight. You must take advantage of this incredible offer right now, or I will have to go ahead and call the next name on my list."

Romel: "Well, uhh, what do I have to do?"

Caller: "Absolutely nothing."

Romel: "Well, sure, I'll take the motorcycle."

Caller: "You <u>are</u> a smart shopper. We will need to collect for shipping and handling, and we can put that on your credit card. What was that number?"

Romel: "I'd rather not put it on my credit card."

Caller: "It's much easier for us if you do, and you'll receive your motorcycle much faster if we get this processed tonight!"

Consumer Law

Analyzing 4-9 (continued)

Romel: "Oh, okay, let me get my card."

Narrator: "Romel's next credit card statement contained a charge to Acme for 'shipping and handling' in the amount of $300. Six weeks later Romel received in the mail a child's bike with a tiny motor. There was no marketing survey included."

1. Did the caller commit an unfair or deceptive sales practice? Explain.

_____

_____

_____

_____

_____

2. How might Romel have handled this differently?

_____

_____

_____

_____

_____

3. What can Romel do now?

_____

_____

_____

_____

_____

Basic Concepts 4-10

Match each definition in the column on the left with the appropriate term in the column on the right.

1. _____ An agreement between at least two persons to exchange something of value

2. _____ The means by which a right is enforced or the violation of a right is prevented or made up for

3. _____ A proposal to do something or pay an amount in exchange for something

4. _____ Agreement to the proposal of another

5. _____ When the two parties agree exactly to the terms of the agreement

6. _____ Something of value

7. _____ Of legal age without mental disability or incapacity

a. acceptance

b. consideration

c. contract

d. legally competent

e. mutual agreement

f. offer

g. remedy

Applying Knowledge 4-11

Review the law on minors and contracts in the text on pages 287-288 and then decide whether or not the minor can cancel each of the contracts below. Give reasons for your answers on a separate sheet of paper.

1. Dan, who is 17 years old but looks like a 20-year old, signs a contract for a $1,000 stereo system from Cascade Stereo. The contract requires him to put $300 down and pay $50 monthly. He puts his $300 down and after two weeks decides he wants out of the contract. Can he legally do this? Give your reasons.

2. Tinh, who is 16, enrolls in Garner Vocational School. She borrows $2,000 from a bank to go to school. The bank has a written statement from Garner School that Tinh is enrolled. Two months later, Tinh wants to drop out of school and cancel her loan. Can she legally do this? Give your reasons.

3. Miguel, age 16, is a star baseball player at his high school. A baseball scout for a professional baseball team approached Miguel and proposed that Miguel sign a contract to play for the team he represents. To encourage Miguel to sign, he gives Miguel a new car. Miguel signs the contract. Later, Miguel realizes that this will deprive him of his amateur status. Miguel now wishes to cancel the contract.

4. Jemi, who is 17, agrees with a married couple who are not able to have children to be artificially inseminated and to bear a child for the couple. The couple will pay all expenses of pregnancy, actual medical expenses and attorney's fees to draft a contract to establish that the child produced will belong to the married couple. Jemi signs such a contract, is impregnated and now changes her mind and wants out of the contract. Can she cancel the contract? Give your reasons.

5. Toni buys a secondhand car for his 17th birthday from Al's used car lot. Toni needs the car to get to his after-school job. After 3 months of use, Toni decides he wants to cancel the contract, return the car and get his money back. Can he do that? Give your reasons.

6. Lam at age 17 buys a used car on credit, paying $50 each month for three years. When he turns 19, two years after signing the contract for the car, he decides to cancel the contract and get his money back. Can he do that? What are your reasons?

7. Miriam, who is 17, set up her own business making T-shirts. She took and filled many orders for sets of T-shirts. She now wants to cancel her contracts that she hasn't filled because she has spent the money on other things and doesn't have enough money to produce the T-shirts. Can she do that? Give your reasons.

Expressing Your Opinion 4-12

The law called "Statute of Frauds" requires that certain types of contracts must be in writing to be enforceable in court. A contract for the sale of real estate is one type of contract covered by the "Statute of Frauds." Consider the following situation and answer the question that follows.

The House Sale

Carmen wants to sell her house. Dale contacts her after meeting her at a party, since he is looking for a house in her neighborhood. They discuss the matter over the phone. Then Dale comes over and they reach an agreement on a price of $85,000. Carmen agrees to fence the backyard as part of the deal, and to replace the roof. They do not sign a contract.

Carmen goes ahead and hires a contractor to fence the yard, and work on the roof. Two days after the work is started, Dale calls to say that he is backing out on the deal, because he is being transferred to another city. Carmen has spent $750 so far.

What is a fair result to this situation?

_____

_____

_____

_____

_____

_____

_____

_____

_____

_____

_____

_____

_____

_____

_____

Basic Concepts 4-13

Match the terms below with their definitions. Then plot the words below on the word puzzle around the term "IMPLIED WARRANTY."

AS IS	FULL
BREACHED	LIMITED
CANCEL	MERCHANTABILITY
CONTRACT	PUFFING
DISCLAIMER	REMEDY
FITNESS	TITLE

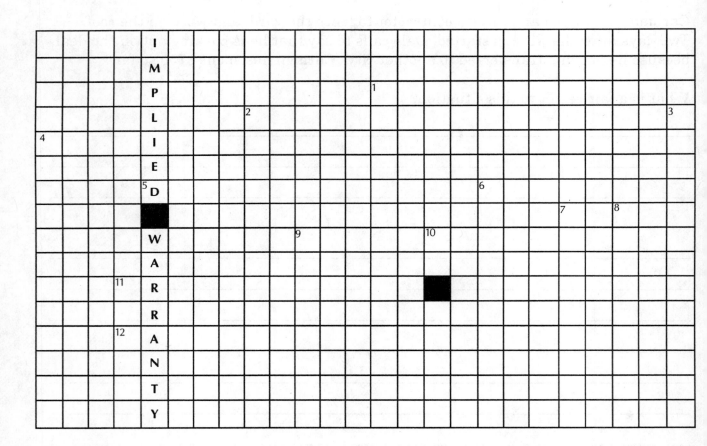

Basic Concepts 4-13 (continued)

Across:

4. Exaggeration or opinion of seller

5. An attempt to limit the seller's responsibilities should anything go wrong with a product

9. A seller's unwritten promise that a product will do what it should

11. Failed to fulfill one's legal duty

12. To make something no longer valid

Down:

1. Legally binding agreement

2. This type of warranty means defective products will be fixed or replaced free; no unreasonable demands will be made on the consumer to get warranty service; reasonable time for fixing the product will be set; replacement or refund after a reasonable number of failed repairs will be made; and notice will be sent to all owners during the warranty period.

3. What is done to make up for a legal injury

6. An implied warranty that the product sold will meet the special need or use of the consumer

7. Less than a full warranty

8. An implied warranty that the seller has the legal right to sell the product

10. A valid way for a seller to avoid one of the implied warranties

Analyzing 4-14

Review the information on warranties in the text on pages 290-294. Read the two warranties below and answer the questions that follow on a separate piece of paper.

Electric Fruit Juicer

This product is warranted for one year from date of purchase to be free of mechanical and electrical defects in material and workmanship. The manufacturer's obligation hereunder is limited to repairing such products during the warranty period, *provided the product is sent prepaid to an Authorized Service Station.*

This warranty does not cover (a) normal wear of parts, (b) blender containers, (c) glassware breakage, or (d) damage resulting from any of the following: negligent use or misuse of the product, use on improper voltage or current, use contrary to operating instructions, or disassembly, repair or alteration by any person other than an Authorized Service Station.

Return of the Owner Registration Card is not required for warranty coverage. This warranty gives you specific legal rights, and you may also have other rights which vary from state to state.

1. What parts and repair problems are covered?

2. Are any expenses excluded from coverage?

3. How long does the warranty last?

4. What will you have to do to get repairs?

5. What will the company do if the product fails?

6. Does the warranty cover "consequential damages"? Consequential damages are other losses caused by the product's failure. For example, if your freezer breaks and all your food spoils, the loss of the food would be consequential damages.

Analyzing 4-14 (continued)

Television

This television is warranted to the original consumer purchaser of this television set that all transistors will be free from defects in material and workmanship for ten years from date of purchase.

This television is warranted to the original consumer purchaser of this television set that all component parts (except those noted in the Warranty Limitation Section below) will be free from defects in material and workmanship for two years from date of purchase.

During the first year of the foregoing limited warranties, the manufacturer will (at its option) repair or replace any defective component part or transistor at no charge to the original consumer purchaser for either parts or labor.

To obtain warranty service, return this television set to an authorized Service Facility with proof of date of purchase.

This limited warranty does not cover: antennas, cabinet, cabinet parts, knobs, batteries, and accessories; cartage or shipment to or from an authorized Service Facility; new products purchased or service performed outside of the United States; uncrating, set up or installation; adjustments of customer operated controls; repairs or replacement parts supplied by other than an authorized Service Facility; any defect, malfunction, or failure caused by or resulting from improper service, maintenance or repair, or from abuse neglect, accident or any other cause beyond the control of the manufacturer, or any product whose serial number shall have been removed, altered, replaced, defaced or rendered illegible. This limited warranty is made only to the original consumer purchaser of this television set and is effective only upon presentation of evidence of provable date of purchase.

No person, agent, distributor, dealer, service facility or company is authorized to change, modify or amend the terms of this limited warranty in any manner whatsoever, except to the extent provided herein in, the manufacturer makes no warranty, either express or implied, regarding this television set including any warranty of merchantability or fitness for a particular purpose and all such implied warranties are limited to the duration of the express warranties contained herein. The manufacturer shall not be liable to the purchaser or to any other person for any incidental or consequential damages or loss of profits or product resulting from any defect in or malfunction or failure of this television set. Some states do not allow limitations on how long an implied warranty lasts or the exclusion of incidental or consequential damages, so the above limitation and exclusion may not apply to you.

This warranty gives you specific legal rights, and you may also have other rights which vary from State to State.

Analyzing 4-14 (continued)

1. What parts and repair problems are covered?

2. Are any expenses excluded from coverage?

3. How long does the warranty last?

4. What will you have to do to get repairs?

5. What will the company do if the product fails?

6. Does the warranty cover "consequential damages?"

7. Does the warranty cover only the original purchaser as opposed to any owner within the warranty period?

Analyzing 4-15

Review the law on disclaimers of implied warranties on pages 294-295 of the text. Then, on a separate piece of paper, answer the questions that follow.

The Corvette

Thomas is looking for a sports car, and sees a used 1976 Corvette Stingray at Al's Used Cars. After looking over the car, he inquires whether a wavy patch of paint means that the car has been wrecked and repaired. Al responds that as far as he knows the car has not been wrecked. Al also tells Thomas that the car is in "top condition" and is therefore priced above the blue book value. Thomas buys the car. At the time of sale, Al asks Thomas to initial the following statement as part of the sales contract: "I understand Al's does not provide any warranties whatsoever, and the auto is sold as is and with all defects..." Al tells Thomas that this provision is to protect him from buyers who punishingly drive high-performance cars like Corvettes and then complain of engine problems.

After driving the car for a week, Thomas notices that it vibrates severely in front, and drifts to the right. He complains to Al, but Al is unable to fix the problem. After driving the car a few months, Thomas finds that the tires are wearing out very quickly. Finally, after five months, the car breaks down.

When Thomas takes the Corvette in to another mechanic, the mechanic notices that the car's frame had been welded, an indication that the car had been previously wrecked.

Thomas takes the car back to Al and demands his money back, plus the cost of the repairs he made to the car. Al points out the provision that Thomas initialed and denies any responsibility.

1. Is the provision a disclaimer?

2. How does it affect Thomas's right to recover from Al?

Name_____ Date_____

Basic Concepts 4-16

Select the terms from the list and write them in the blanks that will make the statements correct.

account	interest
borrower	lost
collateral	money
company	name
credit	pay
creditors	privilege
debtors	repaid
default	secured
finance charge	unsecured
goods	value

1. Using _____ means buying _____ or services now in exchange for a promise to _____ in the future.

2. People who lend _____ or provide credit are called _____.

3. People who borrow money or buy on credit are called _____.

4. A _____ is the additional money over the amount borrowed for the _____ of using credit.

5. Finance charges are based on _____ and other fees.

6. Two types of credit are _____ and _____.

7. Secured credit means consumers must put up some property of _____ called _____ as protection in the event the debt is not _____.

8. A _____ who does not make the required payments is said to _____ on the loan.

9. For protection, any person with credit cards should keep the following information: the _____ of the _____ issuing the card; the _____ number on each card; and the name to call if the card is _____ or stolen.

Name_____ Date_____

Investigating 4-17

Review the *Federal Equal Credit Opportunity Act* on pages 311-312 of the text. Then investigate the laws and agencies that protect persons from credit discrimination in your state. Find out what the agencies are, where they are located and what types of credit discrimination cases have been filed recently. Report your findings below.

_____

_____

_____

_____

_____

_____

_____

_____

_____

_____

_____

_____

_____

_____

_____

_____

_____

_____

_____

_____

_____

_____

_____

Ideas for Community Service Learning 4-18

- Write a consumer law pamphlet for students, or the elderly, on how a specific consumer problem is handled in your state.

- Make videos illustrating how to handle different consumer problems.

- Make a video or write a play about minors and contracts.

- Assist in cross-age teaching of consumer issues relevant to younger kids.

- Write a "consumer help" column in the student newspaper.

- Develop a coloring book for younger students that demonstrates smart shopping ideas.

- Rate grocery stores in your neighborhood and distribute the results to the community.

Family Law

Chapter 5

Vocabulary Building: Word Search 5-1

Review the vocabulary terms in the Family Law Chapter to help you unscramble the words below. Then find the vocabulary terms in the word search puzzle and circle them. Finally, on a separate piece of paper, write a sentence using each vocabulary term.

1. CEORIDV   __ __ __ __ __ __ __

2. EAPRTYINT   __ __ __ __ __ __ __ __

3. ETANIRSAPO   __ __ __ __ __ __ __ __ __

4. IAMYGB   __ __ __ __ __ __

5. INECSTSESEI   __ __ __ __ __ __ __ __ __ __ __

6. IOAYNML   __ __ __ __ __ __ __

7. LOMINPYA   __ __ __ __ __ __ __

8. NNNEMTLUA   __ __ __ __ __ __ __ __

9. NRAIECIHNTE   __ __ __ __ __ __ __ __ __ __ __

10. ODCUTSY   __ __ __ __ __ __ __

11. PNOEMTIAANIC   __ __ __ __ __ __ __ __ __ __ __ __

12. RGORATUES   __ __ __ __ __ __ __ __ __

13. TELNCGE   __ __ __ __ __ __ __

14. TNDAOPIO   __ __ __ __ __ __ __ __

15. TTOIHIABNAO   __ __ __ __ __ __ __ __ __ __

Vocabulary Building: Word Search 5-1 (continued)

```
C  Q  X  E  M  P  W  O  I  P  V  H  Y  N  H
Z  E  E  I  S  J  M  S  N  P  J  W  D  O  N
Z  N  M  V  L  U  N  W  O  Y  E  U  O  I  E
R  Q  D  P  O  E  B  C  I  O  C  Y  T  T  C
T  S  U  R  R  O  G  A  T  E  N  A  S  A  E
C  E  O  X  K  S  L  L  A  Q  A  N  U  P  S
E  P  A  T  E  R  N  I  T  Y  T  N  C  I  S
L  A  D  C  D  O  R  M  I  B  I  U  B  C  I
G  R  O  D  I  P  N  O  B  H  R  L  I  N  T
E  A  P  F  V  E  O  N  A  Z  E  M  G  A  I
N  T  T  Q  O  E  B  Y  H  U  H  E  A  M  E
P  I  I  C  R  Z  Z  F  O  N  N  N  M  E  S
U  O  O  H  C  T  S  E  C  N  I  T  Y  W  K
G  N  N  H  E  P  A  L  I  M  O  N  Y  K  C
R  Q  T  U  L  B  X  H  O  I  H  G  Y  T  Q
```

Expressing Your Opinion 5-2

Circle the words that you believe must be included in the definition of a family, then answer the questions below.

children	aunt
marriage	grandparents
friendship	loyalty
legal obligations	support
household	love
blood relation	encouragement
adoption	development
uncle	custody

1. What words would you add to this list?

_____

_____

_____

_____

_____

_____

_____

2. Based on the words that you select, write a definition of "family."

_____

_____

_____

_____

_____

_____

_____

Basic Concepts 5-3

Match each definition in the column on the left with the appropriate term in the column on the right.

1. _____ A child who misses school without justification

2. _____ The point at which a child is set free from the legal control and custody of parents or guardians

3. _____ Statutes that require adult children to care for needy elderly parents

4. _____ Acts for which children but not adults can be punished

5. _____ Law makes parents/guardians responsible for damages caused by any driver in the family

6. _____ Acts that inflict or threaten to inflict intentional physical, emotional, or sexual harm on a child

7. _____ Failure to properly feed, clothe, shelter, educate or provide for medical needs of children

8. _____ People with government permission to care for minors who are not their own children

9. _____ Legal process by which adults become the legal parents of another person

10. _____ Women who are artificially inseminated for infertile persons

11. _____ Professionals who help married people work out problems

a. adoption

b. child abuse

c. child neglect

d. emancipation

e. family car doctrine

f. family responsibility laws

g. foster parents

h. marriage counselors

i. surrogate mother

j. status offenses

k. truant

Applying Knowledge 5-4

Match the program from the list below with the appropriate definition.

Aid to Families with Dependent Children

Food stamps

Medicaid

Medicare

Social Security Disability Benefits

Social Security Retirement

Social Security Survivor's Benefits

Supplemental Security Income

1. _____ Federal program to pay money for needy people aged 65 and older, the blind or those that have a disability that prevents employment for a year or more

2. _____ Federal program that pays money to workers, aged 62 and older after retirement

3. _____ Federal program that pays money to workers who are blind, injured or too ill to work, if the disability is expected to last 12 months or result in death

4. _____ Federal program to provide money to help poor families in which one parent has died, left home, or is physically or mentally unable to fulfill parental duties

5. _____ Federal health insurance program for people aged 65 or older, people of any age with permanent kidney failure, and certain disabled persons

6. _____ Federal program that pays families when a worker dies and is like an insurance policy

7. _____ Federal program that provides needy persons with coupons that can be exchanged for food

8. _____ Federal program that provides medical services to poor persons

Analyzing 5-5

Read through the hypothetical and answer the question that follows. Write your answers on a separate piece of paper.

Bob and Carol want to marry. Recognizing that they are both strong-minded individuals, with certain goals in mind that might cause problems within the marriage, they decide that it would be wise to decide as many issues as possible before they marry.

They visit the office of Regina, an attorney who specializes in family law. They ask her to draw up a prenuptial agreement for them. This agreement, which means "before marriage" should set out in advance how they intend to handle certain issues that they contemplate will arise during the marriage. It is important that they both are fully honest with each other about what property they own, and any other matters that will affect the marriage.

Bob and Carol tell Regina that they are both 19, and have just graduated from high school. Bob plans to attend college next fall. He has saved $1,000 working as a salesperson at the local hardware store. He has also just inherited $20,000 from his grandmother.

Carol has just started working as a salesperson at Nostrums, a local department store. She would like to become a buyer for the store, and will be enrolled in the store's training program for buyers next year. She will work full-time while she is being trained. The training program requires that she travel occasionally, and once she completes the program, she will probably have to move to another state in order to take a position as a buyer in another Nostrums store. Carol's parents gave her a new car when she graduated from high school.

Bob and Carol would like to have a family, once they have both completed their career training.

What issues should they talk about?

Analyzing 5-6

Read through the case study and answer the questions below on a separate piece of paper.

Kelly and Leon have dated for six months. They are legally of age to marry. At the beginning of their sexual relationship, Kelly told Leon that she has a disease that makes her infertile (unable to have children). Leon insists that Kelly use birth control anyway. Leon does not use any form of contraception.

Kelly becomes pregnant. Leon asks her to have an abortion, since he is not ready to marry, and has plans to go to college. Kelly refuses. They break up, and Leon does not hear from Kelly until a year later, when he is served with papers in a paternity action against him. The suit asks that he be declared the father of the child, and pay support of $350 per month. It also asks for reimbursement of Kelly's medical expenses during the pregnancy, and for past support for the last six months, since the baby was born. Kelly claims that she told Leon after a few months of their relationship that she was no longer using contraceptives.

Leon hires an attorney to represent him because he feels he should not be required to support this child. He denies that Kelly ever told him that she had stopped using birth control.

Leon's attorney argues that Kelly breached an oral contract between them to use birth control. He also argues that her refusal to have an abortion increased Leon's damages caused by her breach of the contract. He also argues that Kelly was careless and negligent in failing to use birth control, and that she intentionally lied to him about whether she was using it.

1. What are the arguments for Leon? Include those in the case study and any you might want to add.

2. What are the arguments for Kelly? Include those in the case study and any you might want to add.

3. How would you rule if you were the judge? Give your reasons.

Expressing Your Opinion 5-7

Read through each hypothetical situation and write on a separate sheet of paper, if you think the partners in each situation should be able to marry. Explain your answers.

1. Sambath is 17 and Sangin is 14. They have known each other since they were small children, and care about each other very much. Their parents have agreed that they should marry. Should they be able to get married now? Why, or why not?

2. Eric's wife died 10 years ago. He has seven children. Since his wife died, he has depended on his first cousin, Sarah, to help with the cooking and cleaning. Sarah is about to graduate from high school and wants to leave home. Eric has decided that he will marry Sarah, so that she will stay and help him take care of the other children. Should he be able to marry Sarah?

3. Vinh and Mai are 18, and have been dating for a year. Mai becomes pregnant. Vinh does not want to get married. Mai's father finds Vinh and forces him at gun point to marry Mai. Should Vinh be forced to marry Mai?

4. Sirhan came to the U.S. 3 years ago with his wife Sisi. In his native country, men were allowed to have more than one wife. Sirhan would also like to marry Carla. Should he be able to marry Carla when he already has a wife?

5. Carlos and Anna decide to get married one night at a party where they have been drinking. They ask their friend Marco to marry them at the party. Marco, a college student, performs the ceremony. Should this be considered a legal marriage? Why or why not?

6. Na, who is 21, kidnaps Muanghin, 15, from her parents' home one night. He takes her to his family's home, where she stays for 3 days. They are then married. Should this marriage be considered legal?

Expressing Your Opinion 5-8

Which of the following factors do you think is most important to a marriage? Number the factors below starting with "1" in order of importance, then answer the question that follows.

_____ religion

_____ money

_____ sexual relationship

_____ common interests

_____ romance

_____ faithfulness

_____ age difference

_____ love

_____ getting along with relatives and in-laws

_____ being from the same culture or native country

_____ children

Why did you rank these factors as you did?

_____

_____

_____

_____

_____

_____

_____

_____

_____

Investigating 5-9

Find out the following information about marriage laws in your state (you may contact the local marriage bureau) and fill in the blanks.

1. To apply for a marriage license in your community, the man and woman must be at least _____ years old. If one of them is only _____ years old, they may marry with the consent of a parent or guardian.

2. Someone cannot be forced to get married. In other words, both parties must _____ to be married.

3. First cousins can get married in your community. Is this statement true or false? _____.

4. To apply for a marriage license, you must go to the: _____ and pay $_____.
   The license is valid _____ days from the date of application.

5. Three people who can legally perform a marriage ceremony are:

   _____

   _____

   _____.

Investigating 5-10

Investigate what state agency handles child abuse cases. Determine what the numbers of cases of abuse and neglect in your state have been in the previous twenty years, previous ten years and in the present year. Determine what the agency predicts will be the future incidence of abuse and neglect in ten years. Chart your findings on the graph below.

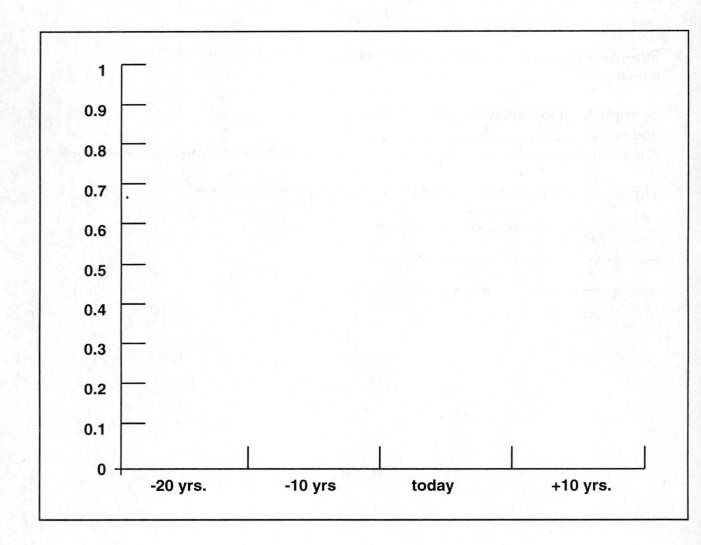

Investigating 5-11

Determine who gets real estate (land and houses) and other property when a person dies in your state without a will (called intestate). You may wish to contact the probate court in your area.

_____

_____

_____

_____

_____

_____

_____

_____

_____

_____

_____

_____

_____

_____

_____

_____

_____

_____

_____

_____

_____

_____

_____

_____

_____

_____

_____

_____

Ideas for Community Service Learning 5-12

- Volunteer to work in a battered women's shelter or a children's shelter.

- Interview immigrant students about families from their home country.

- Adopt a family through a profile and assist the members throughout the year.

- Establish a mentor program at school for new students.

- Research, write and distribute a guide to community resources for abuse victims.

- Research child abuse laws and develop a play, video, or written guide to educate peers or younger children.

- Research AIDS issues. Educate peers with a video, play or guide.

- Raise funds or volunteer for an AIDS hospice.

Housing Law

Chapter 6

Vocabulary Building: Word Search 6-1

Find the following words in the word search puzzle, and then, on a separate sheet of paper, write a sentence using that word.

CONDOMINIUM	COOPERATIVE	ESCROW
EVICTION	FIXTURE	HOMELESS
LANDLORD	LEASE	MORTGAGE
REDLINING	RELEASE	REPAIR
STEERING	TENANT	UPKEEP
WAIVE	WASTE	ZONING

```
E  L  E  C  E  M  O  R  T  G  A  G  E  J  C
R  Z  S  Y  V  U  R  E  D  L  I  N  I  N  G
U  E  S  T  I  I  H  P  K  S  T  W  O  D  T
T  T  E  N  T  N  H  U  L  Z  H  O  R  L  U
X  S  L  A  A  I  E  V  I  A  W  O  Q  X  Z
I  A  E  N  R  M  E  E  H  B  L  W  K  O  G
F  W  M  E  E  O  P  L  Y  D  N  M  N  N  G
Y  Q  O  T  P  D  H  E  N  N  Y  I  O  N  E
B  H  H  P  O  N  O  A  Q  Z  N  I  I  B  R
L  X  N  N  O  O  L  S  A  G  T  R  Y  I  F
Y  X  W  B  C  C  D  E  U  C  E  V  A  E  Y
U  P  K  E  E  P  O  Z  I  E  L  P  Z  T  T
H  O  H  M  G  C  V  V  T  W  E  K  N  X  R
T  Q  E  F  S  A  E  S  C  R  O  W  F  Z  W
E  N  I  L  D  E  R  E  L  E  A  S  E  H  V
```

Applying Knowledge 6-2

Fill in the name of the federal or state law that is described in each sentence below.

1. _____ Federal law preventing lenders from routinely rejecting loan applications from persons attempting to buy a home in poor and minority neighborhoods

2. _____ Federal law preventing discrimination in the sale, leasing, or financing of housing based on race, color, religion, gender or national origin

3. _____ Federal law providing funding for shelters, permanent housing, job training, education, and health care for the homeless

4. _____ State or local laws setting minimum standards for repairs and living conditions within rental units

Basic Concepts 6-3

Review the terms below. Then write the term in each blank that most accurately fits the statement.

application
escalation clauses
evict
lease
month-to-month lease
rent control
security deposit
tenancy at will
tenancy for years

1. Prospective tenants will generally be asked to fill out a lease _____.

2. A _____ is a legal agreement in which the landlord and tenant agree to their rights and responsibilities.

3. Many times, leases require the tenant to pay a _____ to cover damage caused by the tenant.

4. A _____ usually enables a tenant to leave after 30 days' notice.

5. In a _____, the rental is for an indefinite period and the tenant may leave or be told to leave at any time.

6. In a _____, the rental is for an agreed upon time, during which the terms may usually not be changed without agreement of the landlord and tenant.

7. Landlords may generally _____ a tenant who fails to pay rent as agreed.

8. _____ are terms in a lease that provide for automatic increases in the rent during the term of the lease.

9. _____ limits how much landlords can raise the rent.

Expressing Your Opinion 6-4

Read through the two articles — one for and one against rent control. Answer the questions which follow on a separate sheet of paper.

For Rent Control

Housing is a fundamental right, one of the human rights guaranteed to everyone. Providing financial assistance to tenants with low income is absolutely necessary because the amount of affordable housing is declining and the number of tenants is increasing. Tenants are mostly poor, live in substandard housing and pay very high proportions of their income for rent.

Rent control is necessary to protect people who, through no fault of their own, would be priced out of decent housing. The fact that over 200 localities in the United States currently have some form of rent regulation, and more than ten percent of all rental units in the country are subject to rent control, shows that rent control is a good idea.

Additionally, rent control is good because it reduces the frequency with which people move. People care about their neighbors and they feel a loss when a long-time neighbor moves away. Rent control promotes stability.

Against Rent Control

Rent control is not limited to people who are poor. The majority of renters are not poor and the majority of low-income renters live in adequate housing. Rent control is not necessary to achieve adequate housing, since it could also be achieved by providing households with rent assistance financed by broad-based taxes.

Owners of rental property carry a heavy burden. There is a false assumption that landlords make excessive profits. Studies have shown that there are many low-income owners and many high-income renters. Additionally, rent control costs money to administer.

The difficulty of finding a controlled unit leads many tenants to live in units that are not well suited to their current circumstances.

Landlords of rent control properties pay less to maintain the property than of non-controlled properties.[1]

1. What are the arguments made in each article?
2. Are there any arguments that you can add to both articles?
3. Which position do you favor and why?

_____

[1] Arguments were taken fro U. of Virginia School of Law John M> Olin Foundation: Symposium on Law Economics of Local Government: :Is Rent Control Good Social Policy," 67 Chi-Kent L. Rev 931 (1991).

Investigating 6-5

Find out whether or not your community or anywhere in your state has rent control. Then answer the questions below.

1. Ask three adults for their opinions on rent control. Are they in favor of it? Why, or why not?

_____

_____

_____

_____

_____

_____

_____

_____

2. Do you agree or disagree with their opinions on rent control? Explain.

_____

_____

_____

_____

_____

_____

_____

_____

Name_____ Date_____

Analyzing 6-6

Read through the following case and answer the questions that follow.

Al, a recent graduate of law school, is looking for an apartment in a town where he is employed as a lawyer for a legal services organization. Al specializes in housing law, and represents tenants in cases against landlords.

Al responds to Lou's advertisement for an apartment. When he meets with Lou and fills out an application, he puts under "Employment": "Attorney, Legal Services, Landlord-Tenant." Lou tells Al that he has no apartments available, even though he had said on the telephone that he had three empty apartments. Al, suspecting discrimination, sends a friend the same day to ask about an apartment. Lou tells the friend that he has three apartments available.

Al brings a lawsuit against Lou, claiming that Lou discriminated against him because he is a lawyer, well informed about his rights. When Lou hears about the suit, he admits that he refused to rent to Al because he feared that Al would stir up the other tenants, and because he would prefer to have less well-informed people as tenants.

1. Why is Al suing Lou the landlord?

   _____

   _____

   _____

   _____

2. What is Lou's response to Al's lawsuit?

   _____

   _____

   _____

   _____

3. Who should win? Give your reasons.

   _____

   _____

   _____

   _____

Analyzing 6-7

Consider the following situations, and decide whether you think the action in each situation violates federal law. Give your reasons. Write your answers on a separate sheet of paper.

1. Carlos owns a 6-unit apartment in a downtown area. He has three vacancies, and needs to fill them as soon as possible. Jeff and Dirk, students at a city university, are looking for an apartment. They see Carlos' ad and come by to see the apartment.

   a. Carlos tells them the apartments are all rented. He says this because he has had problems with students in the past.

   b. Carlos, needing desperately to rent the apartment, tells them they may rent it, but must pay a $600 deposit, on top of the usual $300 deposit that he charges other students.

   c. Jeff and Dirk are homosexuals. Carlos refuses to even talk with them.

2. Kai-Lin and Frank live together, but are not married. They respond to an ad in the paper for a house to rent in the neighborhood near where they both work. They come by to view the house, and the owner questions them about whether they are married, what their incomes are, and how long they have known each other. The owner finally tells them that the house is already rented.

3. T.D., a quadriplegic and confined to a wheelchair, is looking for a place to live with wheelchair access. There are only two apartment houses in the town that are accessible and with parking close enough for T.D. to get from his van to the apartment easily. Saul, the owner of both apartments, is willing to rent to T.D., but refuses to reserve a parking space close to the apartment for T.D., or to allow T.D. to widen the doorway to the bathroom for his wheelchair.

Basic Concepts 6-8

Indicate who is responsible for the tasks below by circling either **L** for Landlord
or **T** for Tenant or **L** and **T** for both.

1.   L   T   Gets monthly rent

2.   L   T   Must make repairs for misuse

3.   L   T   Decides to allow or not allow sublease

4.   L   T   Signs lease

5.   L   T   Pays cleaning deposit

6.   L   T   Must clean common areas like hallways

7.   L   T   Inspects apartment

8.   L   T   Does routine cleaning

9.   L   T   Makes major repairs

10.   L   T   Pays property tax

11.   L   T   Ensures quiet enjoyment

12.   L   T   May evict for nonpayment of rent

13.   L   T   Owns fixtures regardless who bought them

14.   L   T   May withhold rent in some states if major repairs not made

15.   L   T   May not discriminate on basis of race, color, religion, gender,
             national origin, handicap, having children under 18

16.   L   T   Has right to quiet enjoyment

17.   L   T   Must notify that major repairs are needed

18.   L   T   Fills out application

19.   L   T   Must comply with housing codes

20.   L   T   Pays rent

21.   L   T   Requires security deposit

22.   L   T   Is responsible for wear and tear

Analyzing 6-9

Assume that you are a housing placement officer at the Municipal Housing Authority. The Authority administers a federal program which subsidizes rent for "qualified individuals and families." It is Monday morning and you have a room full of prospective tenants. You must interview them and decide who should have priority for the three subsidized apartments that are available. Using the following definition of "qualified individuals or families," decide who should receive the three subsidized apartments. Write your decisions and reasons on a separate sheet of paper.

To be qualified for subsidized housing, an individual or family must meet the income guidelines, which are that the individual must make less than $14,000 per year, for a household of one person. The income amount goes up slightly as the number in the household increases. If the individual or family meets the income requirements, they are given priority if they meet any of the following additional criteria:

- Homeless with children;

- Homeless without children;

- Living in substandard housing;

- Living in overcrowded housing;

- Paying more than 30% of income for rent;

- Displaced involuntarily from other housing.

1. Theresa, a single mother of three, is unemployed and receiving welfare. She is looking for a job, and has been staying at a temporary shelter for the last month. Her annual income from welfare is $5000.

2. Umberto, is 75 and lives in a building that was just sold to be converted into condominiums. He receives Social Security, but cannot find anything in the newspaper that he can afford to rent. His annual income is $11,000.

3. Sam is an American Indian, and has two teenage sons. Sam is presently renting a studio apartment which is very run down for $300 per month. He wants the boys to have their own rooms, and to live in a nicer neighborhood. Sam makes $5.00 per hour as a dishwasher. His annual income is $12,000.

Analyzing 6-9 (continued)

4. Chung, an 18-year old student, left home after a disagreement with his parents. He is looking for an affordable apartment since he only has a part-time job at a grocery store after school. He is presently staying at his aunt's house, but she has told him that he can only stay one more day. His annual income is $8,000.

5. Su-Lin, who recently came to this country from China, is working as a waitress. She has one child, and cannot find an apartment she can afford, in a neighborhood where she feels safe. She is presently staying with another family. There are three adults and four children living in this one bedroom apartment. Her income is $10,000.

Reflecting on Your Experiences 6-10

Write on the following topic. Describe a time that you saw a homeless person. Identify where you were, what the person was doing, and how you felt at the time and later after the encounter. Describe what, if anything, happened between you and the homeless person.

_____

_____

_____

_____

_____

_____

_____

_____

_____

_____

_____

_____

_____

_____

_____

_____

_____

_____

_____

_____

_____

Ideas for Community Service Learning 6-11

- Research homelessness and its causes. Identify ways to assist homeless people in your community.

- Research landlord-tenant law. Make a video or guide on the rights and responsibilities of a tenant.

- Identify housing resources for needy families in your community, and assist a family in finding their way through the "system."

- Assist *Habitat for Humanity* in building a house for a homeless family.

- Serve as a volunteer "tester," to determine whether landlords in your area are breaking the law by discriminating against prospective tenants.

Individual Rights and Liberties

Chapter 7

Vocabulary Building: Word Search 7-1

Use the definitions to help you unscramble the vocabulary terms. Then find the vocabulary terms in the word search puzzle and circle them.

1. __ __ __ __ __ __ __ __ __   CAGTIMYILE is the status of having been born to married parents.

2. __ __ __ __ __ __ __ __   EALNIGEA is the status of not being a citizen and residing in the U.S.

3. __ __ __ __ __   EAVGU means not clear or specific enough.

4. __ __ __ __ __ __ __ __ __   EIGTNPICK is a permissible union act to publicize a labor dispute.

5. __ __ __ __ __ __ __ __ __ __   EPRNCSSIHO is governmental review of material for the purpose of prohibiting it.

6. __ __ __ __ __ __ __   ERALEDF pertains to the national government.

7. __ __ __ __ __ __ __ __ __ __ __   RORBEVDAHTE is overinclusive.

8. __ __ __ __ __   GASLO are a target of the number of minorities in job positions.

9. __ __ __ __ __ __   HEPCES means the communication of thoughts and ideas.

10. __ __ __ __ __ __ __ __ __ __   IBNSNECETA is the complete refraining from sexual activity.

11. __ __ __ __ __ __ __ __ __ __ __ __ __ __   IOTNIIIRCSADNM is classifying people into groups.

12. __ __ __ __ __ __   KETISR is a union practice of quitting work to force the employer to accept a union demand.

13. __ __ __ __ __ __ __ __ __ __   LTSIBDIIAY is a physical or mental impairment.

14. __ __ __ __ __ __ __ __ __ __   MNETAOADFI is false expression that injures another's reputation.

15. __ __ __ __ __ __   NCTIEO is one of the criteria of due process.

16. __ __ __ __ __ __   NIMCEO is one's salary or wages.

Vocabulary Building: Word Search 7-1 (continued)

17. ___ ___ ___ ___ ___ ___ ___ ___ ___ NIOBTSECY is expression that treats sex in a lewd way.

18. ___ ___ ___ ___ ___ ONNIU is an organization of workers to negotiate with employers on conditions of work.

19. ___ ___ ___ ___ ___ ___ ___ ___ ___ ___ ___ SEECNREPRFE is a way to address past discrimination through favoring one group that has been excluded in the past.

20. ___ ___ ___ ___ ___ SETAT is one of the component commonwealths of the United States.

21. ___ ___ ___ ___ ___ ___ ___ ___ ___ TDMMEENAN is a change.

22. ___ ___ ___ ___ ___ TQOAU refers to a required specific number of minorities in a certain employment position.

23. ___ ___ ___ ___ ___ ___ ___ ___ ___ VCRASEEEN is termination from employment.

24. ___ ___ ___ ___ ___ ___ ___ VICRAPY is the right to be left alone.

```
A  B  S  T  I  N  E  N  C  E  C  I  T  O  N
B  U  Y  C  A  V  I  R  P  M  O  D  G  U  O
O  E  S  A  T  O  U  Q  I  H  I  I  X  N  I
V  C  E  L  B  C  T  G  C  A  Y  S  N  I  T
E  N  C  I  P  O  N  E  K  V  T  A  O  O  A
R  A  N  E  I  W  E  X  E  A  I  B  I  N  N
B  R  E  N  H  P  M  P  T  G  N  I  T  B  I
R  E  R  A  S  V  D  P  I  U  E  L  A  L  M
E  V  E  G  R  F  N  E  N  E  C  I  M  E  I
A  E  F  E  O  E  E  M  G  N  S  T  A  E  R
D  S  E  O  S  D  M  O  K  E  B  Y  F  K  C
T  Y  R  X  N  E  A  C  A  S  O  N  E  I  S
H  X  P  H  E  R  M  N  I  S  G  A  D  R  I
D  D  V  Y  C  A  M  I  T  I  G  E  L  T  D
B  S  G  O  A  L  S  R  F  E  T  A  T  S  W
```

Individual Rights and Liberties

Analyzing 7-2

Read the quotation from one of President Carter's speeches. On a separate sheet of paper, answer the questions that follow.

> America did not invent human rights. In a very real sense, it's the other way around. Human rights invented America. Ours was the first nation in the history of the world to be founded explicitly on such an idea. Our social and political progress has been based on one fundamental principle: the value and importance of the individual. The fundamental force that unites us is not kinship or place of origin or religious preference. The love of liberty is the common blood that flows in our American veins.
>
> — President Jimmy Carter

1. What does Former President Carter say about human rights and America?

2. What does he say is the basis of American social and political progress?

3. What does he say unites all Americans?

4. Give examples that show how America values the individual.

5. What are the problems and benefits of the American system?

6. If you are originally from a different country, compare your country with the United States.

Basic Concepts 7-3

Match each of the terms from the list below with the appropriate description.

a. censorship
b. commercial speech
c. establishment clause
d. fighting words
e. free exercise clause
f. gag order
g. amendment
h. libel

i. obscenity
j. overbreadth
k. prior restraint
l. public forum
m. slander
n. symbolic speech
o. time, place, and manner restriction
p. vague

1. _____ A state law makes it a crime to speak indecently.

2. _____ One city requires all demonstrators to keep off busy streets.

3. _____ The legislative for one town declared that Christianity is its official religion.

4. _____ One city banned any speech that defamed or otherwise included negative information about the city leaders.

5. _____ Students wear a red ribbon to show their support for AIDS-infected persons.

6. _____ Members of the Muslim faith may worship in the United States.

7. _____ A city makes it a crime to make videotapes of children engaging in sexual acts.

8. _____ The Constitution has had additions.

9. _____ Because of the fear that the police officer would not get a fair trial, the court did not allow the media to cover the trial.

10. _____ Because she is unhappy with her performance evaluation, GiGi tells her co-worker that her boss has sexually harassed her.

11. _____ City parks and outside of city hall are places where the public has always been able to demonstrate

Basic Concepts 7-3 (continued)

12. _____ An African-American scholarship club is just finishing a meeting when a white student walks up to one of the members and says, "Get out of here dumb nigger."

13. _____ During the Iraqi War, the government did not allow the media to get access to its battle plans.

14. _____ Students falsely write in an underground newspaper that a specific teacher is an alcoholic.

15. _____ "Buy 3 CDs and get a fourth one free!"

16. _____ The government forbids a newspaper to print the directions for making a hydrogen bomb that the newspaper obtained from an informant.

Analyzing 7-4

Read the facts in the case below and answer the question that follows. Be sure to review the "Expression In Special Places" section on pages 30-34 in the text.

One school district adopted a policy requiring its high school students to submit to school officials for approval all student-written material before any such material could be distributed on school premises or at official school functions. The policies were directed at student writings that were not contained in official school publications.

After the policy had been in place for a few years, students in a high school within the district distributed copies of an unauthorized student-written newspaper called *Bad Astra*. It was given out at a school-sponsored senior class barbecue on school grounds without submitting the publication to officials for review. In addition, a parent, the president of the P.T.A., put copies of the newspaper in faculty and staff mailboxes.

The paper included articles written by the five students that were generally critical of school administration policies, a mock teacher evaluation poll, and poetry. There was no profanity, obscenity, defamatory, or commercial material. Some of the teachers described in the mock poll were emotionally upset with their descriptions. Additionally, the students did not sign their real names to the articles.

The principal reprimanded the students for violating the review policy, but also indicated that, had the paper been submitted for review, it would have been approved. The students, with their parents, sued the school district, claiming that the school policy violates the First Amendment rights of free expression.

How should the judge rule? Give your reasons.

_____

_____

_____

_____

_____

_____

_____

_____

_____

_____

Expressing Your Opinion 7-5

Read through the facts and opinions one and two. On a separate sheet of paper, identify the arguments in each opinion. Write down which opinion you agree with and why.

Facts: One state adopted a "Creationism Act," which requires balanced treatment of creation and evolution science in public elementary and secondary schools. The law forbids the teaching of the theory of evolution unless accompanied by instruction in the theory of creation science. The Act does not require the teaching of either theory unless the other is taught. It requires that each shall be taught as a theory, rather than as proven scientific fact.

It defines the theories as "the scientific evidences for creation and evolution and inferences from those scientific evidences." While not included in the final version of the law, during the drafting of this law, creation theory was defined to include the belief that the elements, the galaxy, the solar system, life, all the species of plants and animals, man, and all things and their processes and relationships were originally created from nothing and fixed by God. Also during the drafting of this law the following inferences of creation science were included, although later deleted: (a) the sudden creation of the universe, energy, and life from nothing; (b) the insufficiency of mutation and natural selection in bringing about development of all living kinds from a single organism; (c) changes only within fixed limits or originally created kinds of plants and animals; (d) separate ancestry for man and apes; (e) explanation of the earth's geology by catastrophism, including the occurrence of a worldwide flood and (f) a relatively recent inception of the earth and living kinds.

The experts who testified in the state legislature on behalf of creation science made these points:

a. There are only two scientific explanations for the beginning of life — creation and evolution science. Both are true sciences, and both present a theory of the origin of life and subject that theory to empirical testing.

b. The body of scientific evidence supporting creation science is as strong as that supporting evolution.

c. Creation science is educationally valuable and can be taught without reference to religion.. Students exposed to it better understand the current state of scientific evidence about the origin of life.

Expressing Your Opinion 7-5 (continued)

d. Although creation science is educationally valuable and strictly scientific, it is now being censored or misrepresented in the public schools. Evolution is misrepresented as an absolute truth.

e. The censorship of creation science has at least two harmful effects: it deprives students of knowledge and it violates the Establishment Clause. Secular humanism is itself a religion and evolution is a central tenet of that religion.

The stated purpose for this law is to protect academic freedom. A group of parents, teachers, and religious leaders challenge the Act's constitutionality in federal court, claiming that the Act violates the Establishment Clause of the First Amendment.

Law: To determine whether legislation comports with the Establishment Clause, it must pass a three-pronged test, called the Lemon test:

1. The legislature must have adopted the law with a secular purpose. If the law has no secular purpose, the law is unconstitutional.

2. The statute's primary effect must be one that neither advances nor inhibits religion.

3. The statute must not result in an excessive entanglement of government with religion.

Opinion one

The state law is unconstitutional. The primary purpose of the state legislature was to advance the religious viewpoint that a supernatural being created humankind. The leading expert on creation science testified at the legislative hearings that the theory of creation science included belief in the existence of a supernatural creator. The legislative history also documents that the Act's primary purpose was to change the science curriculum of public schools in order to provide persuasive advantage to a particular religious doctrine that rejects the factual basis of evolution in its entirety.

The true purpose of enacting this law is to narrow the science curriculum. Requiring schools to teach creation science with evolution does not advance academic freedom. The Act does not grant teachers a flexibility that they did not already possess to supplant the present science curriculum with the presentation of theories, besides evolution, about the origin of life. Since school teachers can already teach any scientific theory, the stated purpose of academic freedom is not furthered by the law.

Expressing Your Opinion 7-5 (continued)

Out of many possible science subjects taught in the public schools, the legislature chose to affect the teaching of the one scientific theory that historically has been opposed by certain religious sects. The legislature passed the Act to give preference to those religious groups which have as one of their tenets the creation of humankind by a divine creator. The Act is either to promote the theory of creation science, which embodies a particular religious tenet, by requiring that creation science be taught whenever evolution is taught, or it is to prohibit the teaching of a scientific theory, disfavored by certain religious sects, by forbidding the teaching of evolution when creation science is not also taught.

The Establishment Clause forbids alike the preference of a religious doctrine or the prohibition of theory which is deemed antagonistic to a particular dogma. Because the primary purpose of the Creationism Act is to advance a particular religious belief, the Act endorses religion in violation of the First Amendment.

Opinion two

The Creationism Act is clearly constitutional. The legislators considered the potential Establishment Clause problems and went through several drafts of the law in order to approve a final law that articulated the secular purpose they meant to serve. The only evidence in the record on creation science is that it is essentially a collection of scientific data supporting the theory that the physical universe and life within it appeared suddenly and have not changed substantially since appearing. It is a strictly scientific concept that can be presented without religious reference.

The first prong of the *Lemon* test requires that the law have a secular purpose. To determine whether the law has a secular purpose, we must examine the actual motives of the state legislators. The Establishment Clause does not forbid legislators to act upon their religious convictions. We would not strike down a law providing money to feed the hungry or shelter the homeless if it could be demonstrated that, but for the religious beliefs of the legislators, the funds would not have been approved.

The fact that the law coincides with the tenets of some or all religions does not mean that the law's purpose is to advance religion.

The Court's task is not to judge the debate about teaching the origins of life, but to determine what the members of the state legislature believed. Most of them voted to approve a bill which explicitly stated a secular purpose.

They heard the scientific experts give an authoritative basis for including creation as a science. Therefore, this Act has a secular purpose.

Investigating 7-6

Find out whether the state law on discrimination in your state is the same as the federal law, or whether it prohibits discrimination for more reasons than the federal law. For instance, some states have laws that make it illegal to discriminate against people because of their marital status, sexual orientation or status as a student. You could contact the state agency in charge of human rights. On a separate piece of paper, answer the following questions.

1. What organizations in your state or community help people with claims about discrimination?

2. What claims are the most frequently made?

Basic Concepts 7-7

Determine whether each statement is true or false. Indicate your answer by writing
either **T** for True or **F** for False in the space provided at the left. For each statement
that is false, on a separate piece of paper rewrite the statement to make it true.

1. _____ The "right to privacy" phrase is specifically mentioned in the
United States Constitution.

2. _____ The Supreme Court first recognized the right to privacy in a landmark
case in 1855.

3. _____ When the right to privacy conflicts with another right, the right to privacy
will win, because it is a preferred right.

4. _____ Some judges and legal scholars think that the Supreme Court has made
a mistake in protecting privacy.

5. _____ There is no longer any truth to the claim that a person's home is his
or her castle.

6. _____ The constitutional right to privacy protects consenting adult males who
engage in a sexual act in their own home.

7. _____ The constitutional right to privacy protects adults who possess obscene
material in their home for private use.

8. _____ The constitutional right to privacy protects students from having their
school records released without a parent's permission.

9. _____ The Freedom of Information Act has made it possible for the public to find
out about individuals' medical, financial, criminal and employment records.

10. _____ Since the landmark Roe v. Wade decision granting constitutional protection
to a woman in choosing abortion, the U.S. Supreme Court has given states
more power to limit the right to an abortion.

Basic Concepts 7-8

Read through each statement. Circle **S** for Substantive Due Process, **P** for Procedural Due Process or **S** and **P** for both.

1. S   P   Written notice of the proposed action

2. S   P   Personal right to privacy

3. S   P   Assistance of an attorney

4. S   P   Courts substituting their judgement for legislatures' judgement

5. S   P   Notice of an appeal

6. S   P   Right to call witnesses

7. S   P   Right to cross-examine witnesses

Analyzing 7-9

Read through the following case study and, on a separate sheet of paper, answer the questions that follow.

The Jaycees, founded in 1920, is a nonprofit membership corporation for the promotion of young men's civic organizations in the United States. It aims to educate them in the affairs of their community, state and nation and to develop true friendship and understanding among men of all nations.

Regular membership (voting members only) is limited to young men between 18 and 35 years of age. Associate members, who may not vote may, include women and older men. As of August 1981, the Jaycees had about 295,000 members in 7,400 local chapters. At that time women made up about 2% of the Jaycees' total membership (associate members). Jaycees' activities regularly involve men and nonmember women working together.

A regular member, after paying a fee followed by annual dues, is entitled to participate in a wide variety of activities to enhance his individual development, community development and management skills. In taking these classes and then in implementing projects, Jaycees members work with other members, many of whom they have not met before.

Two Minnesota chapters of the Jaycees began admitting women as regular members. As a result the chapters have violated the national organization's by-laws and are facing revocation of their charters. The members of these two chapters file charges of discrimination. They claim that the exclusion of women from full membership violates the state's Human Rights Act, which states that it is unfair discrimination to deny any person the full and equal enjoyment.of the goods, services, facilities, privileges, advantages, and accommodations of a public place because of sex. The Jaycees counter and claim that requiring them to admit women violates the male members' constitutional rights of free speech and association.

1. What are the important facts?

2. What argument are the two chapters making?

3. What argument is the national organization of Jaycees making?

4. What constitutional rights are involved?

5. Whom do you agree with and why?

Analyzing 7-10

Read through the following case study and, on a separate sheet of paper, answer the question that follow.

Mr. Irvis, an African American, was refused service by the Moose Lodge, a local branch of the national fraternal organization. A white member in good standing with the Lodge had brought Mr. Irvis to the Lodge as his guest and requested service of food and beverages. The employees at the Lodge denied him service solely because he is an African American.

The Moose Lodge has a policy and practice of restricting membership to whites and permitting members to bring only white guests on to the premises. The Moose Lodge is a private club. It is a local chapter of a national fraternal organization having well-defined requirements for membership. It conducts all its activities in a building that it owns. It is not publicly funded. Only members and guests are permitted in any lodge. One may become a guest only by invitation of a member or upon invitation of the house committee.

Mr. Irvis claims that his Fourteenth Amendment right to equal protection of the laws has been violated. The Moose Lodge claims that, as a private club, it can determine who it admits as members and guests.

1. What are the important facts?

2. What argument is Mr. Irvis making?

3. What argument is the Moose Lodge making?

4. What constitutional rights are involved?

5. Whom do you agree with, and why?

Ideas for Community Service Learning 7-11

- Research activities of hate groups in your community and devise strategies for students to combat these groups. Keep in mind the right to free speech.

- Present a mock trial to younger students about the Bill of Rights.

- Research and write a synopsis of landmark cases on the Bill of Rights, and make it available for civics classes in your school.

- Conduct a poll of your peers to determine their knowledge and opinions on individual rights. Devise a strategy for educating them on their individual rights and responsibilities under the Bill of Rights.